SCHENNIS

TWEE KEER GRAFSCHENNIS

ns de Heavy Sound-da-
r in de stad een en ander
l, hoewel die zaken nu
et moeten overdreven

Het feit van de graf-
op het oude kerkhof
vandalen een lijk uit de
er en zelfs uit de kist
s zeker een erge zaak.
s er trouwens de oor-
in dat de Poperingse
gesloten werden voor
Sound. Elke betrokken
eft die feiten veroor-
Maar tijdens diezelfde
agen nu nog een tweede
hennis gepleegd zijn op
kerkhof in de Deken.
l.
aak kwam pas aan het
m...eugelum, een
In een
alen (de-
ben een
breken.

SCHADE

Dat er tijdens het
Sound Festival schade werd
gericht aan bepaalde eigen
men is een vaststaand feit

ene bron
re minde
Het is z
«schade
werden
een 30-t
het bedr
zal ligge
«misbru
paalde b
stellen o
organisa
schijnli
al een v
om een
mensen
wens be

organisatoren leefden stipt alle afspraken na, het stadsbestuur was tevreden en gaf onmiddellijk de vergunning voor 1985.

Eventjes zag het er naar uit dat de oppositie er rel rond zocht. Een storm in een glas water.

Ze zouden daarbij eer
schaar gebruikt hebben,
der op het jaar al ontvree
uit het materiaalhokje
kerkhof. De daders
evenwel niet geslaagd
hun opzet. Wijst de hage
er op dat de daders in Pop
en omgeving moeten g
worden? Bij de ordeli
meent men van niet. Het
zoek in deze zaak is e
volop aan de gang. Be
getuigenissen zouden en c
zen dat de feiten gepleeg
den door niet-Poperinge
bangers. Meer informa
men over de zaak niet kw
ieder geval bestempelt me
tweede grafschennis als m
erg.

patrouilleren eigen veiligheids-
diensten. De post ,,person
kosten   veiligheid'' be
300.000 fr., het dubbele va
rig jaar. Daarbij moet no
wat materiaal worden geh
vooral de honderden r
dranghekken.

bouwd dicht
De zenuwkr
de Ouderdo
ders zullen
40 % van de
tenlanders, v

Programm
Met hun pro
organisatoren
een breder p
de stoere hea
ook de zuiver
afzakken. Ev
vorig jaar, zo
meent Luc W

Slayer, de hardste en ruigste band ter wereld. Af en toe worden ze in rockclubs geweigerd. Reden: overdreven gebruik van vuur en rookbommen. Dat belooft voor Poperinge..

Was dit het laatste Heavy Sound Festival?

POPERINGE — Onmiddellijk na het Heavy Soundfestival te Poperinge werd positief gereageerd over deze
manifestatie. Dank zij een uitstekende organisatie had het
treffen een kwasi rimpelloos verloop gekend. Toen een
paar dagen nadien ook een bilan werd opgemaakt van de
gebeurtenissen in de rand van het festival werd deze
aanvankelijke mening herzien. Vijfenvijftig schademeldin-
gen werden genoteerd, er was agressie tegen personen, er
werd graf- en lijkschennis vastgesteld. Zowel bij de overheid, die de organisatie toelaat en derhalve verantwoor-
ding af wil leggen, als bij de organisatoren die aansprake-
lijk worden gesteld voor de schade, duikt de vraag op of het
wel zin heeft en nog mee door te gaan.

Waar vorig de horeca aversie
tegen het festival uitsp
het onge...

aan de legale ordediensten. Pui
werk. Vermits het vaak ove
vreemden ging en vermits de
overheid ervan uitgaat dat deze
vandalen landlopers zijn die
geen vermogen hebben om de
schade te vergoeden en dat derhalve een gerechtelijke proce-
dure weinig op zal leveren, worden de organisatoren recht-
streeks voor .. ateriële scha-
gesteld. Niet
want dat kan
dingen op de
half miljoen
en aan het
aakten. Uit-
rganizato-
security-
n en voor
dt aange-
ders zijn
rden be-
daders.
n zich
borg-
ze hun

Poperings raadslid liet graf openen om foto's te nemen

Poperinge — De grafschennis die een paar dagen na het
Heavy Soundfestival werd vastgesteld, krijgt thans een
staartje. Het juridische onderzoek naar de schuldigen is
nog steeds lopende en daarvan is enig resultaat nog niet
bekend. Aktie wordt er wel gevoerd aan de kant van de Poperingse schepenkollege, want dat beschuldigt CVP-frak-
tieleider d'Udekem van ,,politieke grafschennis''. Op eigen
houtje en zonder enige machtiging liet, twee dagen na het
ontdekken der feiten, d'Udekem een gemeentebediende
ddels dichtgemaakte graf weer openmaken om er
maken, met een flits en niet met fakkels
van het kerkhof niet meteen straf-
el kan deze be-
el om de

werd gezegd dat zoiets niet meteen de bedoeling was. Wel staat
het de prokureur vrij op eigen
initiatief deze aangelegenheid
aan te pakken. Daarom ook
werd ze openbaar gemaakt.

Desgevraagd zei de burgemeester dat een uitslag van het lopende onderzoek over de feite-
lijke grafschennis nog niet is
bekend. Headbangers waren zaterdag aanwezig op het kerkhof.
Duitse hardrockers waren 's a
vonds in de omgeving van het
kerkhof met fakkels op ronde.
Herrie werd gehoord de poli-
chteraf werd de hoogte ge-

it het
is en
elijk
ak-
te
d-
o
n
kan deze be-
neen straf-
bangers ge-
aken om er
gen na het
bediende
ter
aze
lij

storm was slechts lichte bries

gen op
rhalen
die de
werd
na het
t alle-
noeite
en, en
meer
e een
s oms
ook
wie
en
n
aal

Invasie relatief rustig verlopen

POPERINGE. — De invasie van een 7000-tal ,,headbangers''
in de hoppestad is relatief rustig verlopen. Het Heavy Sound
Festival had de dagen voordien nochtans een soort angstpsy-
chose teweeggebracht bij de plaatselijke bevolking en niet in
het minst bij de horeca. Maar echte agressieve uitschieters
zijn er niet geweest. In een stad waar men dergelijke esbatte-
menten niet gewoon is heersten uiteraard het nodige argwaan
en ook wel een dosis nieuwsgierigheid. Zo'n luidruchtige,
excentrieke en non-conformistische bedoening ..
ringe niet elk weekend m

werd deze
als degene
ie hier
verwerpe
eiten
van het
bracht
bezon
deken graf
tive graf-
voeg
a

Heavy Sounds in the West
By Hans Verbeke & Onno Hesselink
www.heavysoundsinthewest.com

Published by:
Heavy Reads & Earth Island Books
www.heavyreads.com - www.earthislandbooks.com
First printing, May 2024, Belgium
© 2024, heavyreads.com

ISBN: 978 19 16 864306

heavy sounds in the west

prelude †

"Ik kan er verdomme een boek over schrijven"*, as we say in West Flanders. And here it is! This book tells the story of the metallic storm that swept the pastures of West Flanders in the 70s and 80s. About the incredible host of bands and artists that blew the dust straight off the region. My home region. They were the first to blow up a speaker around here, with fans and volunteers cheering them on. There was no complaining or whining, they just soldiered on. With unyielding passion and drive.

My childhood friend Danny and I used to hang around the streets of Kortrijk in the late 70s and early 80s. We were about ten years old, cycling past the first hard rock pubs on our custom-built bikes. Somehow, we felt connected with that crowd. Van Halen, AC/DC and KISS — hell yeah, tons of KISS — were the mainstays on the soundtrack of our summer holidays. Man, we were obsessed. It was like KISS fever took over, just like people went nuts for the Beatles in the 60s. At least, that's how it felt. I plastered KISS logos all over my schoolbooks and a lot of friendship books. Danny's book of friends got KISS'ed too. The 'KISS Alive II' LP I got from my mother came with a cool sheet of stick-on tattoos. Our salivary glands worked overtime sticking them all over ourselves. And then there was that extra sheet to join the KISS Army. For two long years, I waited on pins and needles for my black KISS belt buckle to arrive. Still got that bad boy today.

7

* West Flemish proverb, loosely translates as "I could write a goddamn book about it."

Meanwhile, I had got into punk too. As a curious nerd, I was always fascinated by anything that sounded out of the ordinary. I couldn't care less about radio. Hard rock was my first love. In that respect, my mum was a great inspiration. Deep Purple, Uriah Heep and Rainbow got regular spins at our house, but also the Stones and The Beatles. My father was a huge Beatles fan. When my parents separated I suddenly became that "outcast kid of divorced parents" at the strict Sint-Amands College. Divorce, after all, was not done in the 1970s, and most certainly not in a Catholic community. It didn't take long before I hooked up with kids hanging out on the streets. They were clad in faded jeans, had cool pins on their jackets, and soon I knew I wanted to look like that too! The beatings that I sometimes took suddenly became a thing of the past. These

street kids were dangerous. And now I was one of them. The latest revelations like Iron Maiden, Motörhead and Rush arrived through my uncle Koen, a hard rock DJ operating under the moniker Studio 2112. From then on, I swung back and forth between rock and punk, but I still cherish them both.

Today — with double 5 lurking around the corner — I am contributing to this book about my two first loves: Heavy Sounds and West Flanders. This is where the early heavy metal movement first planted its foot firmly on the European mainland. An invasion that would settle itself in our little corner of the world for good. Read on and discover an electrifying piece of rock history laced with West Flanders' entrepreneurial spirit, youthful DIY resolve and, above all, an endless stream of fantastic music. *Hans Verbeke*

prelude ☨☨

I turned six or seven and got to pick out a birthday gift. Every time 'Crazy Horses' blasted out of our dinky transistor radio at home, it blew my little mind. So I chose that single by The Osmonds. "Oowee! Oowee! Crazy Horses..." That tune was like my anthem; I was totally hooked. Next on my musical radar was AC/DC. Hard rock was in full swing by then, and you couldn't go a day without hearing 'Whole Lotta Rosie' on the radio or TV. After dabbling with Van Halen - I even tried to make a cardboard replica of Eddie's guitar - I dived head-first into punk. Suddenly, musical finesse took a backseat. Meanwhile, Bon Scott, AC/DC's frontman, kicked the bucket from excessive drinking, and the Sex Pistols dropped their 'Never Mind the Bollocks' LP, shocking the world - including me. The Pistols blew everything else out of the water, and I couldn't care less about hard rock for a good while. Punk morphed into hardcore with one motto: faster, faster, faster! When that hardcore energy started influencing heavy metal bands, it all came full circle. Metallica, Slayer, and a bunch of others started adding hardcore to the mix, birthing a new sub-genre called crossover. Musical purists debated endlessly: is it metal or is it punk? Honestly, I didn't, and still don't, give a damn. What matters is the lights, sound, drums, guitars ... Let there be rock!

Onno Hesselink

early days

In times long gone, when even Angus was still young, the epicentre of heavy guitars was briefly located in Poperinge. So-called betonmuziek*, a nickname worn with pride, was flown in from places far and wide (AC/DC! Van Halen! Rush!) to the most Western part of Belgium. Much has been written about the famed West Flanders entrepreneurial spirit, but the story of heavy metal in the Westhoek reads like the ultimate case study: falling down, getting up again with stubborn perseverance, endlessly plodding against the grain, followed by unimaginable success and sometimes... the obligatory brutal crash. And the hop farmer, he ploughed on.

15

Burgeoning decibels

Anyone who has outgrown the adolescent stubble knows that there is not much fun to be had without some decent foreplay. And so, at the end of the sixties, there's some light tremors noticeable in the microkingdom of Belgium, well before the big bang of guitars strikes. A thunderstorm hits upon the region for the first time when Jimi Hendrix plays in Mouscron in 1967. That must have been quite a power surge, which is still commemorated with a bronze relief of Jimi. While the electric charge accumulates, the idea of a Euro-Woodstock seems to be crystallising in Kortrijk. However, authorities at the city's Broeltorens broke out in a fearful sweat at the thought of a tsunami of hippies. The festival shifted 25 km east, to Amougies in France, at the foot of the Kluisberg hills. Master of ceremony Frank Zappa kept the 80,000 visitors under his spell and had Pink Floyd, The Nice, Yes, Soft Machine and many others trooping in, spread over five days in October 1969.

The bright skies over the village were starting to rumble with distant thunder. With the embers still smouldering on the meadows, heavy metal entered its formative years. The triumvirate of Led Zeppelin, Deep Purple and Black Sabbath battered many an amplifier in the first half of the seventies. The plan was for Ozzy and his mates to showcase their mayhem at the Hallen in Kortrijk, in January 1974. However, the show got cancelled, and the Kortrijk rock crowd faced yet another letdown after their local Woodstock had already been nipped in the bud.

Fortunately, in 1973 Hawkwind and UFO had already played the venue, and in '74 Irish guitar god Rory Gallagher made his mark there. Anyway, it's not in the West Flemish heavy metal genes to simple give up and frown: if your jacket gets ripped, you just sew on a couple of patches, done. It's onward and upward, my friends! Heavy metal and this region, there seems to be something special in the air. But to unravel what exactly that is, we have to head some forty kilometres deeper into the Westhoek...

Unidentified Flying Object

In 1975, a many-headed hydra called 'ODIL concerts' rose from the dense Poperinge soil. Founded by Eric Deroo, José Verbiese, Bertin Deneire and Patrick Tydtgat, ODIL was short for *Onbekend Ding in de Lucht**: a Flemish ufo looming over the concert landscape. The collective wanted to promote the current pop scene locally at the conference hall of the local swimming pool. Local bands didn't really catch on, but ODIL hung tough. If it didn't work out with local talent, then they'd focus on bigger international acts. A series of dance nights — locally known as t-dansants or TDs (tea dances) — brought in a fair bit of money, which was used to rope in more established bands. Brussels-based hardrock heroes Kleptomania, highly regarded at the time, was one of the first bigger names to hit the town in 1975. In 1976, Kayak from the Netherlands provided the fuse that really lit the powder keg. This happened at the Maeke-Blyde, the soon-to-be concrete hotspot for concrete music.

From then on, the rock really got rolling. Over the following years, acts from all over the globe flew and rode in. In 1976, northern neighbours Focus — remember their yodeling scorcher 'Hocus Pocus'? — crossed the border. In '77 we welcomed The Runaways, with Joan Jett and Lita Ford in their ranks, who were dismissed as 'pussycat rock' in the papers. The idea that *wimmin can't rock* was still very much alive back then. But boy, these gals sure proved them wrong. The Runaways completely ch-ch-cherry bombed the Maeke-Blyde. In 1980, Brit band Girlschool demolished the place, and in 1982 our Belgian metal pride Acid, with caped singer Kate, settled the score once and for all.

The annual bird show

In 1977, ODIL gets the chance to book

16

* Dutch, translates as 'unidentified flying object'

A thunderstorm hits upon the region for the first time when Jimi Hendrix plays in Mouscron in 1967. That must have been quite a power surge, which is still commemorated with a bronze relief of Jimi.

the up-and-coming Aussie band AC/DC. At the time, hardly anyone knew exactly who they were. However, at a meeting in café 't Kantientje, Eric Deroo announced that the band wants to start their European tour in Poperinge. And that it seems like an opportunity not to be missed. But the regular haunt at Maeke-Blyde turns out to be unavailable... because of the annual bird show! So they booked the tiny hall 't Belfort at the Grote Markt instead, up until then only used for t-dansants. They had to rent an extra generator to provide the necessary high voltage. The place was packed, with 900 people crammed into the hall like sardines. According to technician Luc Cleenewerck, the fuse box almost blew under the heavy guitar artillery. His account of the event illustrates the tenacious DIY ethos needed to make shows like these possible.

The papers are full of praise about that oddball Angus Young in his school uniform, with both journalists and punters going apeshit as he bounces through the audi-

ence on singer Bon Scott's shoulders. Stuff like that was unseen at the time. Also unique: people coming all the way from Antwerp and even Paris, hoping to get in without a ticket (it's still 1977, remember?). We don't know how (or if) those poor souls ever made it home.

Abasti concerts
The smell of metal was in the air. And the Westhoek saw a sudden drop in sales of cotton earbuds, as an earwax-popping guitar assault hit the region relentlessly. Inspired youngsters Luc Waeyaert and Rik Stael promptly founded 'Abasti concerts'. They specialised in programming the heavier side of rock, mainly at the Maeke-Blyde. From then on, there was hardly a weekend without live rock music. The stakes were high from the get-go, with a show by Dutch pride Golden Earring as their very first feat. What followed was a seemingly endless stream of concerts, culminating in the legendary Heavy Sound festival—a story told later in this book.

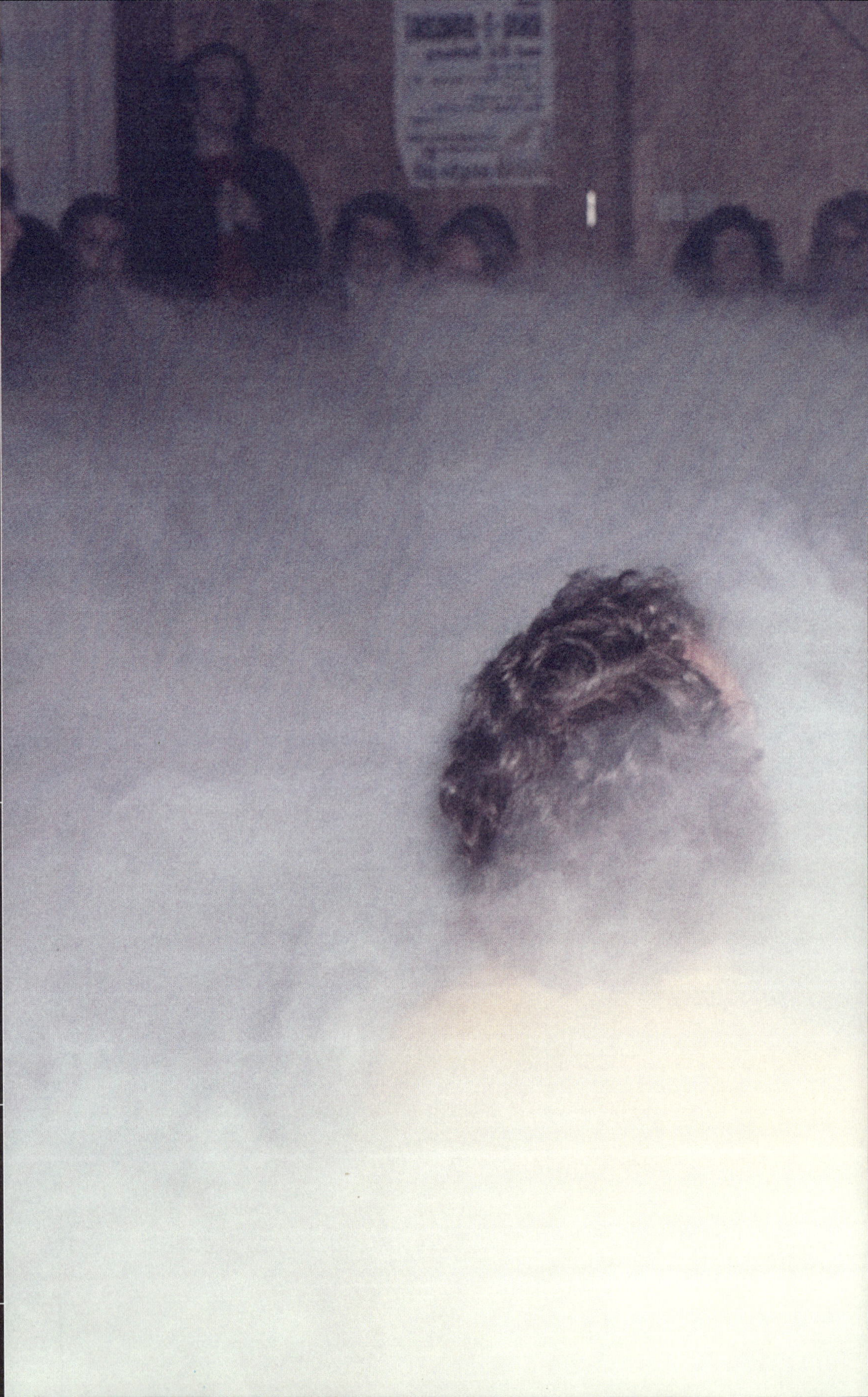

Kleptomania | De Gilde- Poperinge | 01-02-1975

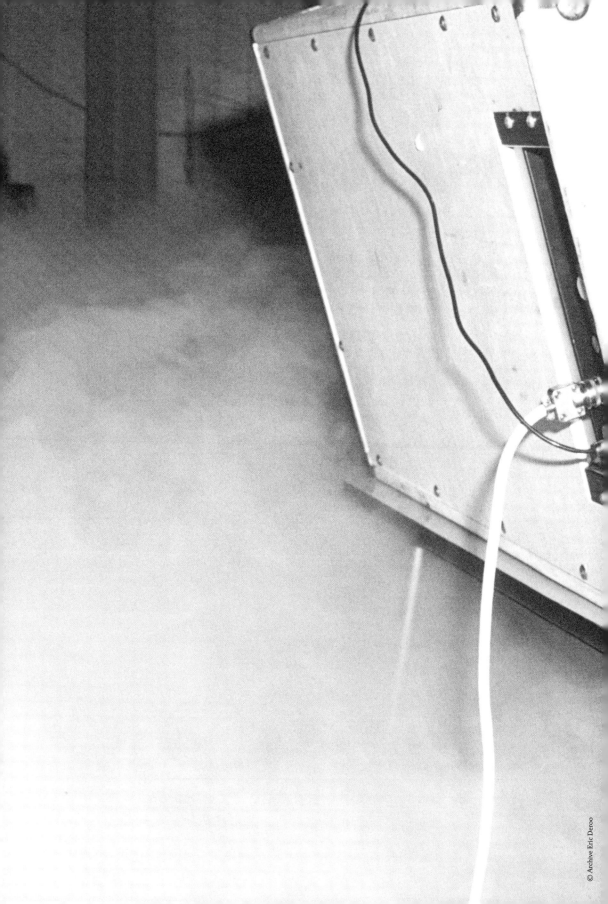

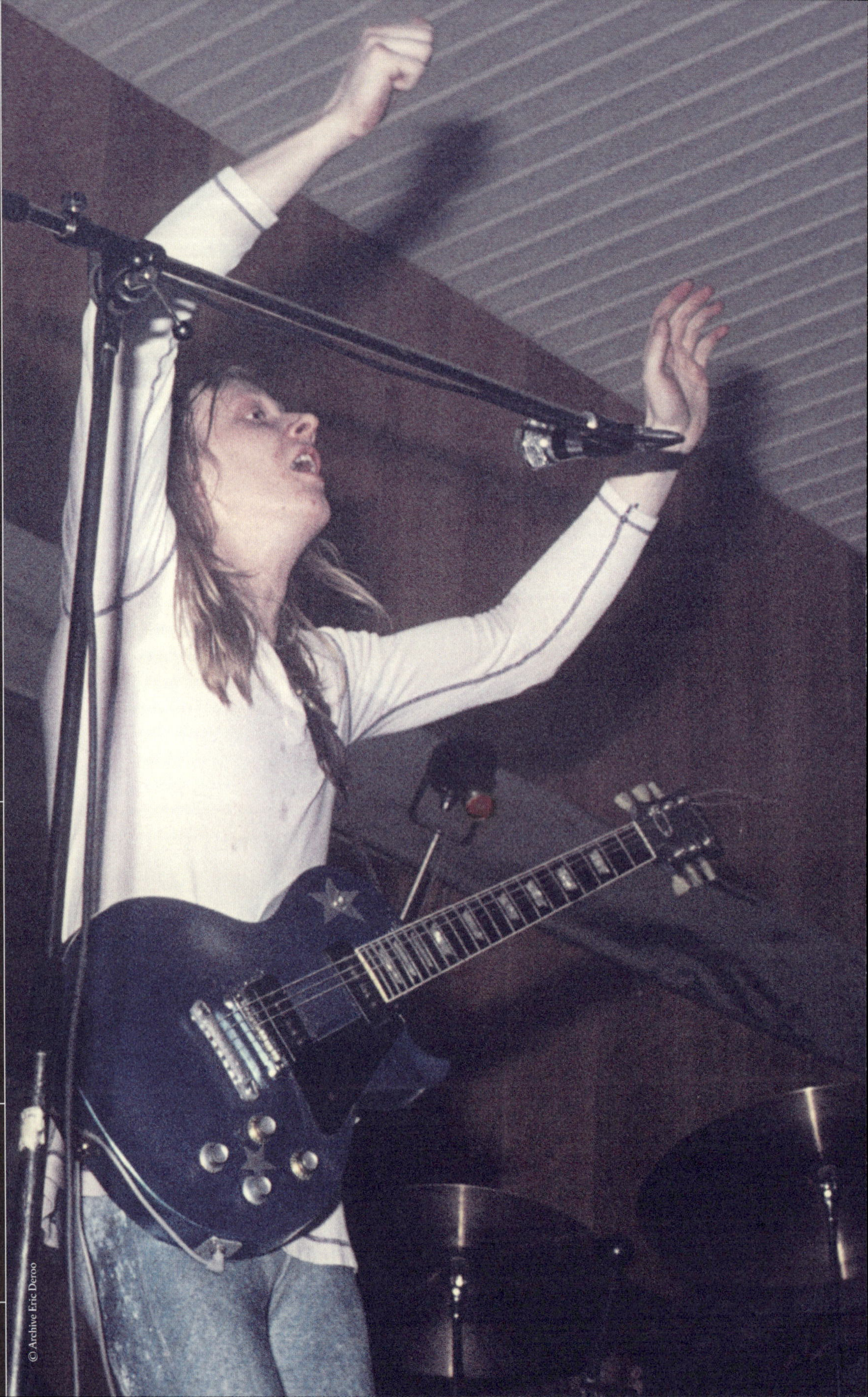
© Archive Eric Deroo

Kleptomania | De Gilde- Poperinge | 01-02-1975

Undoubtedly one of the hottest bands to emerge from Brussels in the early '70s, Kleptomania played their own brand of Sabbath-influenced hard rock. The band's lead guitarist Dany Lademacher - who would go on to join Herman Brood's Wild Romance a few years later - was the main attraction. The show was put on by ODIL in the tiny venue De Gilde Rekhof in Poperinge. Those present describe it as a rock solid show, spiced up with frantic riffing and smoke-spewing machines.

KISS in Harelbeke

ODIL were not the only ones to reach out to the hard rock hordes of Western Europe. Loose initiatives and self-styled concert promoters sprang up like mushrooms. Out of nowhere, in 1976, KISS were booked for a show at the Ontmoetingscentrum in Harelbeke. In that same year, UFO, Ted Nugent and Tangerine Dream would also play at the venue. The story: At the end of KISS' first gruelling European tour, it turned out there was no money left for the band's return trip across the pond. So Harelbeke was chosen as the final fundraiser. But for KISS, already huge in the States, it was to be a bumpy ride. Literally. Throughout the tour, the band had been travelling in senior citizens' coaches, with large windows and stiff-upper-lipped drivers who weren't too keen on the bacchanal going on at the back of the bus. On the way to Brussels, where they stayed at the Hilton the day before the show, the driver refused to stop for a toilet break. We suspect he was more used to transporting children on school trips than having American hellraisers on board. He explained his logic to singer-guitarist Paul Stanley: "It's simple. You drink out of the bottles. You empty them all the way down. And you fill them up again. Problem solved." To which Stanley replied that if the band didn't get to empty their bladders soon, one of those bottles would bluntly hit the back of the driver's head.

The next morning the driver had vanished into thin air. The stage equipment had already been dropped off, so the band embarked on a long, arduous journey by public transport. In their own words, they felt "stuck between West Flanders farmers and chickens on a train, like in a Fellini film". Anyway, KISS blew the roof off the Ontmoetingscentrum that night, fuelled by their own backstage beer bar. And the organisers went the extra mile: they rented special racks to hold KISS' stage equipment and props (weighing around 3000 kilograms per square metre!) and dry ice for their fog machines. Meanwhile, Jacques Merlevede, who owned the Popcenter record shop in Kortrijk, warmed up the locals by promoting the band's latest double album, 'Alive!'

No more than 500 people attended this first Belgian KISS show. But those who did were full of praise. Still, the ceiling of the venue was so low that some adjustments had to be made. There was not enough room to fit in Peter Criss' drum riser. The fireworks and rocket launches from Ace's guitar didn't happen either. But Gene Simmons did get to perform his fire-breathing act, scorching the venue's ceiling. All in all, the band definitely left their mark on Harelbeke and made the crowd hungry for more.

✝✝✝✝✝✝✝✝✝✝✝✝✝

When we finally arrived at the hall they had a keg
of beer and a tap system waiting for us backstage.
We tried to empty that the same night. I also
remember that the venue's ceiling was so low that
Gene blackened it during his fire-breathing act.

Jay Barth, Sound Engineer KISS

✝✝✝✝✝✝✝✝✝✝✝✝✝

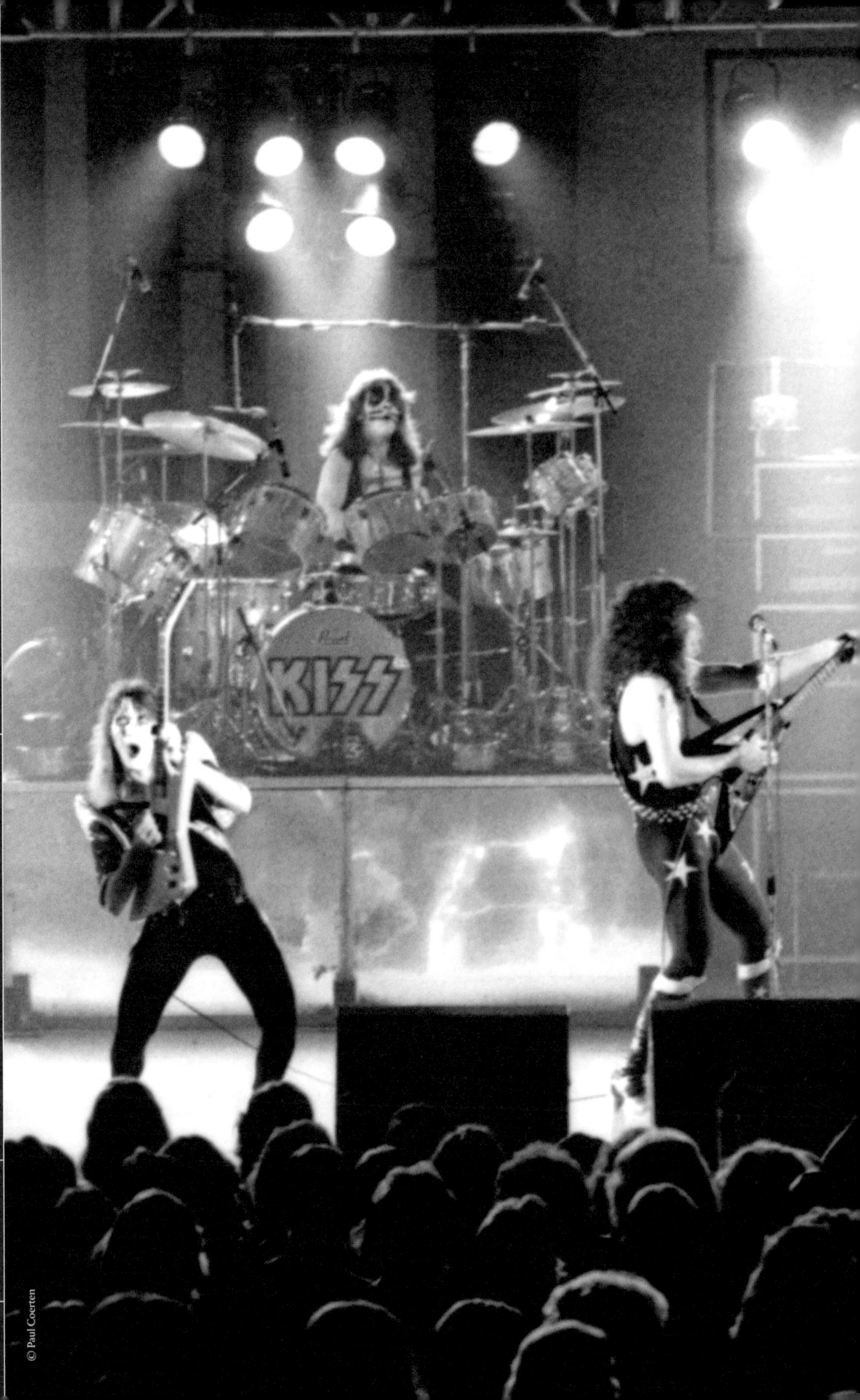

© Paul Coerten

As a true fan, I had followed KISS closely from the very beginning. I remember that first European tour like it was yesterday. They sold out the first show in Manchester and played to more than 2,500 people. The band also toured the rest of Western Europe with Scorpions as a support act. The last show of that tour was at the Ontmoetingscentrum in Harelbeke with barely 500 people attending. It was probably their smallest crowd on that tour, but the Belgian fans were absolutely ecstatic. *P. Shell*

Superfan Marnik Bellecoste with on the left Gene Simmons and the original poster of the concert on June 6, 1976 in Harelbeke.

That first European tour was downright humiliating for us as a band. I was pissed off as soon as we got off the plane. We were already big in the States, but in England and the rest of Europe we had to prove ourselves all over again. We were back to square one, like nobodies. Thank God for the fans who pulled us through. In England the crowds were amazing but the food was terrible and the transport was outdated to say the least. Europe was a bit better in that respect. But the whole tour was run by a bunch of stiffs. There was no air conditioning. And can you believe they only put one single ice cube in your drink over there? *Paul Stanley*

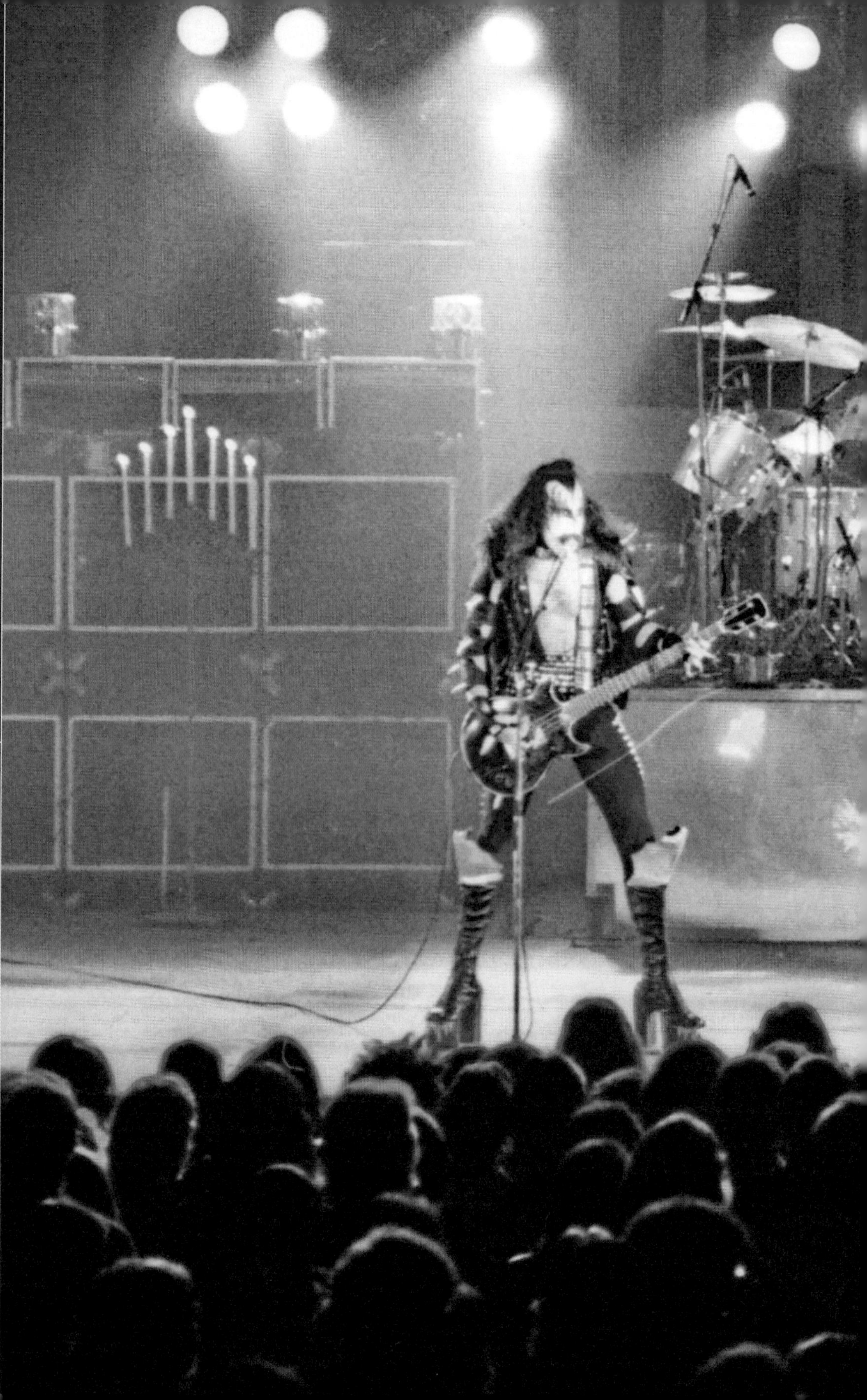

KISS

Ontmoetingscentrum - Harelbeke

06-06-1976

Ontmoetingscentrum - Harelbeke

Ted Nugent

Ted Nugent was on a short promo tour in Germany when we were able to rope him in on a spare day in his schedule. I volunteered that night, but to be honest I'd never heard of the guy. We were told he was quite an eccentric character. He didn't drink and hated cigarettes, both backstage and in the venue. When I brought in some food and drinks for his band and crew, with a cigarette dangling from the corner of my mouth, some cowboy pointed out to me that he wasn't taking any of that shit. I then asked the organisers if that was the band's manager. Apparently, I'd been mouthed off by the Motorcity Madman himself. During his show the man was on fire. I had never seen a guitarist give such a scorching performance. It looked like he had secretly been drinking petrol or something. Unforgettable. *Bertrand Ameye*

© Archive Eric Deroo

The Camel show turned out to be a real nail-biter: during the sound check, Peter Bardens' Hammond organ broke down. This made the proggy Brits nervous as hell. We called in a technician from Ypres who took care of the tube-driven organ. The audience got impatient and the tension grew. In the end the problem turned out to be a loose wire. Slightly euphoric, everything was put back together again. But then the organ began to hum angrily. After a few phone calls, the cause was found and the problem solved with the necessary organ mumbo-jumbo. When Camel returned to Belgium, they brought two Hammonds with them, just to be on the safe side. They obviously remembered their first time in Poperinge... *Eric Deroo, Odil Concerts*

© Archive Eric Deroo

Hocus Pocus in Poperinge

Focus with Thijs Van Leer. That attracted quite a few outsiders. But this time they weren't dressed in leather jackets. No, these odd men out were expecting classical music. Apparently lots of older West Flemings had 'Introspection', Thijs Van Leer's classical flute album, on their shelves. Out of the blue, our college music teacher Roger Orroi also turned up. He became an instant Focus fan, as did many others that evening.

On 19 February 1977, Scorpions from Germany passed through Harelbeke with their latest LP 'Virgin Killer' under their belts. The original album cover shows a nude pubescent girl, her intimate parts barely obscured by a erm... crack in the camera lens. The cover was deemed too controversial for American audiences at the time. 50 years on, it's still on the receiving end of moral outrage. The band itself says the following about it: "It was never an album cover we proudly showed to our parents. There was always disagreement about it in the band. At one point, it caused a scandal on Wikipedia, which ended in a temporary shutdown of the site. Even the FBI got involved.

AC-DC

High Voltage Rock 'n roll

ODIL concerts

ODIL concerts saw the light of day in the early 1970s. This group of young people got together to organise concerts for teens in and around Poperinge. Besides the main crew, there are about fifteen other volunteers who help out with setting up the venue, putting up posters, and handling all the practical stuff.

When I was about 18 years old, I was recruited as technical manager, responsible for electrical matters and supporting the roadies who had to operate the sound and lighting gear. Our meetings were held at 't Kantientje, a popular pub near the St-Jans church, the closure of which I have always regarded as one of the greatest losses to the hotel and catering industry in Poperinge.

It was Eric Deroo in particular who had a nose for up-and-coming talent and for snatching up acts while they were still affordable. Among the first groups booked were Earth & Fire from the Netherlands, featuring the gorgeous Jerney Kaagman on vocals, Kayak and Pink Floyd stalwarts Camel. Later deals were struck with Focus, The Runaways and the young Van Halen.

Most of the concerts took place at the Maeke-Blyde, but sometimes we moved them to smaller venues like the Jeugdheem, the RMS Hall or 't Belfort. Some shows were organised in cooperation with other promoters, such as newcomer Herman Schueremans or Ludo Debruyn of Lion Promotions. The artists themselves usually stayed at the Palace Hotel.

AC/DC

I vividly remember the meeting when Eric Deroo told us we could book AC/DC. To be honest, we had never heard of this Australian band. In fact, I thought the name was rather lame as AC/DC stands for 'Alternating Current / Direct Current'. For someone who was into electronics like me, it was a bit run of the mill.

Eric: "It seems they are very popular with hard rock fans in Australia and they are looking for a place to start their European tour. For that price we can't go wrong..." I think we paid them 40,000 Belgian francs, which is about 1,000 euros. Everyone agreed, although no one really knew what the group was about. Then came the first setback: the Maeke-Blyde hall was already booked for the annual bird show on 8 October. So we had to look for another venue, which turned out to be 't Belfort on the Grote Markt. But it was clear that the technical facilities of 't Belfort couldn't be compared to those of the Maeke-Blyde. Not by any stretch of the imagination.

"What kind of &xxx!@ hall is this?"

Two huge trucks pulled up to 't Belfort in the Veurnestraat with our 'discobar'. The first thing the tour manager mumbled when he saw the venue was "What kind of &xxx!@ hall is this?" After some thought it was decided to unload only half the equipment. So we got to work and soon the entire surface of 't Belfort was covered in flightcases.

The boss of 't Belfort walked around among the cases of equipment and all he could mutter was "goddamn". When the lids came off the huge mixing consoles, he grumbled "goddammit" one last time and just went AWOL for the rest of the evening. Meanwhile, the roadies had started stacking speakers and lighting rigs up to the ceiling.

At one point the head technician tugged at my sleeve to tell me that the rented power generator only supplied 220 volts. Technically that wasn't a problem. All we had to do was switch some plates in the generator cabinet, but... The bloody cabinet was locked and they hadn't left us the key. Patrick Maerten rushed over to the rental company to get it. Meanwhile the band were already in the cobwebbed room under the stage of 't Belfort, downing whiskies. These guys were all remarkably short in stature. *They weren't exactly pretty, weren't exactly tall.* Had evolution stalled in Australia? Anyway, as about 900 tickets had been sold, we started letting the audience in, one by one. But it soon became clear that 't Belfort was going to be far too small.

Packed like herring in a barrel

It was now 8:30pm and the tension in the room was rising. The generator had been adjusted, but everything still had to be fine-tuned. And that took

some time. The audience started to get rowdy, as they were literally packed like herring in a barrel. I remember there was this gorgeous girl with long blonde hair à la Britt Ekland in the front row, wearing a scoop neck sweater and no bra. I asked José Verbiese if he had noticed her too. His reply was: "Mate, I'd stay away from her if I were you, she's with the Hells Angels!"

"The power's going down!"

The concert started about an hour late. Angus Young stole the show, raging like a madman in his typical school uniform with shorts and cap. My own stress peak was yet to come, when one of the roadies suddenly shouted "The power's going down!" You see, we had hooked up the sound system, which was quite big but only used 220 volts and so didn't require a lot of power, to the venue's mains. According to the band's engineers, this should've worked. But when we went to measure the voltage on the venue's oldschool fusebox, we saw the meter indicating 220 volts with no band playing. As soon as the amplifiers were turned up, it dropped to 200 volts, 190 volts, 180 volts,... Believe me, that had us sweating bullets.

I decided to double-check the generator too. When we started it up in the afternoon, it turned out to be very noisy. We were worried that the buzzing would be audible during the concert. When we apologised for this to the tour manager, his response was "No worries, mate. We'll top that!" It was clear that things were about to get loud.

To escape the ear-splitting guitar violence for a moment, I decided to check things again. That's when terror struck me. The power meter hit 90 amps when lighting groups were switched on, while the fuses could only handle 60 amps. We had no spare fuses and an emergency repair was a no-go. If a fuse was blown, there'd still be sound... but no more lights. Miraculously, everything held up just fine. The 900 attendees of one of the most legendary concerts in Poperinge returned home — or headed to one of the city's pubs — with ringing in their ears.

After the show, Young & co went back to the Palace Hotel. When Eric Deroo and I went to say our goodbyes on Sunday morning, Gerard Vroman was still behind the bar. "They emptied our entire supply of liquor. When one of them went to sleep, another one of them got up. We haven't seen our beds yet." Two years later, on 19 February 1980, AC/DC singer Bon Scott would die of acute alcohol poisoning in London. *Luc Cleenewerck*

I was volunteering at ODIL in Poperinge that night, checking tickets at the entrance. Back then, we often had a number of tickets printed twice to mislead SABAM, the Belgian association for authors, composers and publishers. How's that for rock 'n' roll? The venue was packed, there must've been about 900 rabid fans crammed in there. And there was a mob out front, still hoping to a get a ticket. It was a glorious night, to say the least... *Bertin Sanders*

It's been a long time and I was barely 18, so my memories may be a bit hazy. The fact that I'd had quite few pints doesn't help either. 't Belfort — actually just a sports hall — was not suited for this kind of music event at all. The sound was excessively loud and bounced off the walls. Back then, noise regulations didn't really exist.

☩☩☩☩☩☩☩☩☩☩☩☩☩

This was the loudest rock show I ever attended — hands down. I'm wearing a hearing aid these days, something I secretly blame this concert for. They had our ears ringing for days. Never before had we seen, or heard, anything like it.

I don't exactly recall the setlist, but I do remember the wild guitarist, dressed like a schoolboy in shorts and a school cap. For a large part of the set he rode on singer Bon Scott's shoulders, churning out a barrage of riffs and hits. Good times, and I'm still proud I was there to witness that.
Steven Meuleman

There weren't a lot of shows at 't Belfort in Poperinge, and the black fitted carpet on the stage was ridden with mould and other noxious substances. So a few days before the AC/DC show, we had it chemically cleaned. However, the product they used was so strong that it partially dissolved the colouring of the carpet. On the night of the gig, Angus exorcised his demons, writhing and wriggling all over the stage floor. After the gig, Bon Scott had to scrub Angus' sweaty, blackened back clean with a towel. As you can guess, his back turned fiery red, completely irritated. They thought it was hilarious. But I can imagine that, today, we would at least have called the poison control centre. *The ODIL crew*

Maeke-Blyde - Poperinge

© Archive Eric Deroo

The Runaways, a hard-rocking female four-piece from California including Joan Jett and Lita Ford, started making waves in the 1970s. The newspaper articles from the time are, well, quite representative for the time. The journos pointed out that these women just might hold their own with their male counterparts. Of course, they didn't fail to mention that the predominantly male audience would not only get a treat for the ears but there would also be plenty to feast their eyes on. The papers heralded The Runaways as 'Pussycat Rock' with glee, with a sidenote that they were actually a good band too. A first sign of the changing zeitgeist maybe?

Hard rock? Load of bollocks!

Moonfreak played mostly hard rock and AC/DC covers. There weren't many bands like us in the area. So ODIL asked us to open for The Runaways. At the time we were hanging around London a lot, discovering what punk was all about. Jacques Merlevede from the Popcenter record shop in Kortrijk became our manager, and he suggested that we should change the band's name as well as our look. We changed Moonfreak to P.I.G.Z, short for 'Punk Is Grote Zever', which translates as 'Punk Is a Load of Bollocks'. When we played the gig in Poperinge, both the organisation and the audience were shocked. Gone was the hard rock image and music: we had become a full-fledged punk band. Our sound guy Dirk had eaten all our sandwiches backstage, but paid us back in full with a sublime sound mix. Joan Jett wore Yves' skinny tie on stage and thought it was super cool that we covered The Damned's 'New Rose'. *Rik Masselis, P.I.G.Z*

In 1977, the Kortijk-based P.I.G.Z. found themselves at a crossroads between hard rock and punk. Determinedly heading down the punk path, the band wins 'The First Belgian Punk Contest' in Brussels in March 1978.

Our sound guy loves rock 'n' roll too!

We felt blessed when they asked us to open for The Runaways. After all, they were a big name in the hard rock genre that everyone looked up to. I remember it was a Sunday, it was also the first time P.I.G.Z. got to play with a real PA and I was their regular sound guy. The audience was obviously there to see The Runaways. For P.I.G.Z. it was more of a showcase and an incredible first stage experience.

Technically it was an eventful evening. The sound engineer in charge was being a dick. Basically he didn't want to mix P.I.G.Z. I was still a rookie, little did I know about power structures and pecking orders at shows. As a support act, you were always up against the same old song and dance: the guy in control of the PA refusing to cooperate. "*Hey, it's your band. You fix it*". I wasn't used to this kind of high-end equipment, and usually support acts don't get the chance to do a proper soundcheck. So I just left the mixer settings as they were after The Runaways' soundcheck. All in all, it sounded pretty good. But then again, we didn't set the bar too high.

We didn't get paid for the show, but we didn't care. After I moved to Antwerp in February 1978, Jacques from Popcenter took over the band's management. It was he who later got P.I.G.Z. the support slot for Iggy Pop at Forest National, but that's another story. *Dirk Wanseele, sound enigneer P.I.G.Z*

The Westhoek: kingmaker of guitars

I have been a huge Van Halen fan from day one. And a proud member of their fan club for many years. The 1978 world tour in support of their debut album was the American hard rock band's maiden voyage. The tour mainly criss-crossed the States, with 125 shows in the USA and two in Canada. But they also added 38 dates in Europe and 7 in Japan. This added up to a staggering 172 shows over a period of around 10 months, making it one of the most extensive and impressive tours in the band's history. Many contemporary bands would undoubtedly struggle with such a killer pace. Although Van Halen toured mainly as support acts for bands like Black Sabbath and Journey, they often played headline shows in Europe and Japan.

The Poperinge show was unique. The band's very first Belgian show had a modest turnout - hardly anyone knew the band at the time - but the dynamics within the band were incredible. Vocalist David Lee Roth turned out to be a spectacular showman and Eddie's guitar playing was downright insane. You could just feel that this band was going somewhere. *Jan Beverse*

At that time, Poperinge was considered a hard rock mecca, frequented by locals and rock lovers from countries such as Germany and France. At that time - I was 16 or 17 years old - I was able to attend legendary concerts of AC/DC, Rush and many others. My favourite memory is of Van Halen playing just 100 metres from my front door. I could literally hear the show from my bedroom window.

In the 1980s we had Heavy Sound, a hard rock festival unlike any other rock show. For three days, hard rock fans took over the whole town. I vividly remember shops locking their doors, shutters being pulled down and people being downright scared. *Alex Vanhee, Photographer*

The gig had not yet started, but we were already impressed. We marvelled at the immense drum kit with double bass drum. Four bass drums actually, as the support act had brought its own double bass drum too. Amazing! I was in the front row, and not much later David Lee Roth jumped on top of me. I could feel his soaking wet, bare chest and I loved it. *Frank Holvoet, Definitivos*

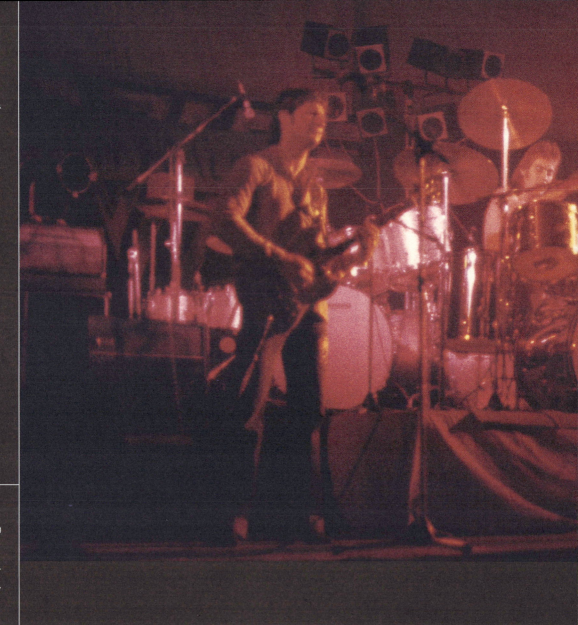

Atomic Punks

On 4 May 1977, St. James got the chance to open for Van Halen, who were still relatively unknown over here. But they did already have that rock star attitude. Their self-titled first LP had just been released and they were about to embark on a world tour. The band was completely shielded, it was impossible to even get near them. Nevertheless, they gave us backstage passes and we were allowed to see a bit of their soundcheck, under the watchful eye of two roadies/musclemen. We were totally blown away by Eddie's unseen guitar technique and the massive sound.

© Archive Eric Deroo

Then AC/DC played the Arena Hall in Deurne on 26 October, with us as support act. The day after, we played with AC/DC again, in the sports hall in Koekelare. The contrast to Van Halen couldn't have been greater. Those Aussies were really down to earth. We mingled with the band in their dressing room, these guys had no stuck-up attitude at all. I remember Bon Scott guzzling whisky and Angus conscientiously sticking to mineral water. They even asked us to join them on tour, which started the following day in London. Unfortunately, as some of us already had day jobs, this never happened. Something we still regret to this very day. *Noël Oyen*

Rush at the airport

By 1979, Rush had already achieved cult status with the elaborate and epic style they perfected on albums such as 2112 and Hemispheres, and the tours that accompanied them. Through his connections, Eric Deroo of ODIL Concerts approached the band's booker and the Canadian trio was booked to play a show in Poperinge. Tickets sold like hot cakes, thanks in part to the efforts of Popcenter's Jacques Merlevede, who ran a promo campaign similar to the one he did for the KISS gig in Harelbeke three years earlier. A week before the show, however, a telex arrived from Rush's management: the band would play a second show in Paris instead of Poperinge. Eric panicked, but decided not to say a word to the team. 'Speech is silver, silence is golden': that's old West Flemish pub wisdom for ya.

When he finally dropped the bomb a few days later, all the posters for the show were taken down, ticket sales were immediately stopped and Jacques was asked to give people their money back. Not much later another telex arrived: "Rush will play in Poperinge, Belgium". Full stop. Under reluctant grumbling, posters were put up again and people were asked if they didn't want to spend their refunded money. Apparently Rush would be flying from Paris to Lille, a last-minute plan that ODIL had to accommodate. Jacques and his sidekick Johan were sent to the airport as a welcoming committee. In an attempt to reduce stress, nail biting and cognac consumption at the airport bar were taken to unprecedented levels that day. As a parade of business suits stepped off the plane, there was no sign of the Canadian rockers. Until suddenly a number of long-haired characters appeared: the gig could go on after all.

Rush played an impressive show in front of 1,300 fans. Before heading on to Scandinavia, the band's busy tour schedule allowed them a few days off. However, Jacques and Johan had other plans. They decided to take Geddy, Alex and Neil on an adventurous pub crawl in Kortrijk. Not all stories are suitable for publication, but the tour must have been legendary. The events culminated on the stage of De Stovebuis café, where casual passers-by were treated to the 'performance' of a motley crew of rockers.

┼┼┼┼┼┼┼┼┼┼┼┼

I'm still proud that we managed to get Rush in 1979, despite the bumpy ride. The band has only played in Belgium twice in their 50-year career: here in Poperinge and in Brussels.

Eric Deroo, ODIL Concerts

┼┼┼┼┼┼┼┼┼┼┼┼

Maeke-Blyde - Poperinge

Max Webster

64

© Archive Eric Dervo

✝✝✝✝✝✝✝✝✝✝✝✝

Don't get caught in the Rush
to see Max Webster

✝✝✝✝✝✝✝✝✝✝✝✝

De Krimson café

Usually the young folk from Menen would head to Kortrijk for a night out, but sometimes a delegation from Kortrijk would come to us for the weekend. Café De Krimson in Menen was definitely one of the roughest hotspots in those days. You could get just about anything there, including a nasty beating if you asked for it. The Menen gang ran the place. They were actually a bunch of hoodlums who used to bust up scout parties, but once they made a name for themselves, it stuck like a bozo at the bar on a Saturday night.

I remember a little French bloke in an AC/DC shirt coming in for a pint. He was going to the toilet when two gang members followed him in, probably to harass him. By the time the toilet door swung back open, the guy had floored his attackers and finished his beer.

But in the end we all got on well. Whenever there was trouble, it was usually because some drunken idiot was harassing the ladies in our company. Etienne, the bar manager, kept an unloaded riot gun under the bar, which he would occasionally pull if the situation was about to escalate. No one dared stand up to Etienne. The guy was a fucking legend who had been bringing big names to West Flanders since the 1970s... UFO, Maiden, you name it. De Krimson was close to the barricades at Menen station. The locals really hated it. They crossed the street when they passed the bar and kept their distance. De Krimson had no windows, they were all nailed shut with wooden boards. At one point the Menen authorities tried to close it down, but to no avail. *Steven - Steffe Blackie*

Motörhead bombs Poperinge

When I was about seventeen, I discovered Motörhead through a compilation of harmless blues and soft rock acts. But that one Motörhead track set me on fire, without even knowing what the band looked like. When I heard about their gig in Poperinge - I lived nearby in Veurne - I jumped on my moped and picked up my mate Mark for a rough ride through fields and back roads.

With some bravado and a touch of bluff, we wormed our way into the unguarded backstage area. The deafening volume of the support act provided the perfect cover to sneak into the band's dressing room. Before I knew it, there I was - pint in hand - watching the Motörhead guys booze themselves into oblivion. Even before the show there was chaos and mayhem backstage, with the road crew constantly struggling with sound and power problems.

The gig itself was a raw, unrelenting maelstrom of sound. Subtlety was nowhere to be found as the band put on a crushing stage act. The noise was so extreme that I could barely make out the songs. With every riff, the concrete hall shook under the blistering volume. Three ominous figures going full throttle, without giving a single fuck about the audience... I thought that was übercool.

And then there was Lemmy. Dressed in his trademark black shirt and bullet belt, snarling into the mike that hovered above him like a weapon. The ultimate headbanging madness. Like a musical hurricane raging through the hall. I loved it. This concert is still high on my top 10 list. You can be sure that I'll be a fan until my very last riff. *Francis Verwee*

Maeke-Blyde - Poperinge

Motörhead

Maeke-Blyde - Poperinge

Motörhead

✝✝✝✝✝✝✝✝✝✝✝✝✝

The gig was a raw, unrelenting maelstrom
of sound. Subtlety was nowhere to be found
as the band put on a crushing stage act.
The noise was so extreme that I could
barely make out the songs.

Francis Verwee

✝✝✝✝✝✝✝✝✝✝✝✝✝

Wheelpop Festival
Kortrijk - 5 April 1980

Later in this book we claim that Heavy Sound was the first metal festival on the European continent. But, in reality Wheelpop might win that claim to fame. Seemingly endless semantic discussions aside - was it hard rock or metal? - the city of Kortrijk was shaken to its foundations in 1980. Once again, it was the illustrious Jacques Merlevede of the Popcenter record shop who had his finger firmly in the pie. The Wheelpop organisation had grown and was able to rope in Judas Priest as the headliner. There was hardly a bigger name in the genre at the time. After Ian Gillan, Iron Maiden played their first European show there, and they didn't even have an album out yet.

Judas Priest pulled out of the festival at the last minute, and the rented Harley that Rob Halford was supposed to ride onto the stage had to be cancelled. Up until the last minute, people at the box office were wondering who was going to replace them. In the end, Nazareth filled in for Priest,

causing quite a stir among ticket-holders. The young Iron Maiden made up for a lot though. They even met their future drummer at this gig. Nicko McBrain was drumming with McKitty that day, a power trio whose guitar broke down halfway through their set. While technical problems were sorted out, McBrain's minute-long bass and drum solo wowed the audience and Iron Maiden alike. When drummer Clive Burr was kicked out of Maiden two years later, McBrain stepped in to beat the skins.

↓↓↓↓↓↓↓↓↓↓↓↓↓

Forty years ago, after my first two months in the army, I was granted a weekend off. I jumped on the first train and headed off to the Wheelpop festival in Kortrijk. All friendly people there, but we didn't understand one iota of the West Flemish variant of Dutch. Nevertheless, we had some hilarious conversations.

I was there as a stagehand and also manned the box office. I don't remember who was pulling the strings at the festival, maybe Tienne Vanneste or Louis Soubry. I'm pretty sure it wasn't just Jacques from Popcenter who was in charge. Financially, he didn't have the means to take the lead. But when it came to handing out tasks and making decisions, he definitely called the shots.

After the set-up, I kept the box office, which was outside the venue in the Halls, open until the early evening. Unfortunately this meant that I missed most of the shows, apart from Nazareth and the Ian Gillan Band. I can't remember if I saw Iron Maiden. Probably not. I had no idea who they were back then. What I do remember is a lot of people without tickets coming up to the box office asking who was replacing Judas Priest. There was a bit of a com-motion about that. Some bought tickets any-way, others left disappointed. A few demanded refunds, but I wasn't allowed to give people their money back, which led to even more dis-content and discussion. *Dirk Wanseele*

╀╀╀╀╀╀╀╀╀╀╀╀╀

Wheelpop is where I first saw Iron Maiden. *Iron who?* They were still an unknown band at the time... I was speechless after the gig and became a fan for life! Their first album had-n't even been released in Belgium yet. I got it from friends for my birthday two months la-ter. A fantastic record. That night Nazareth played one of the loudest shows I've ever been to, fronted by screamer Dan 'Expect No Mercy' McCafferty, of 'Ears Hurt' (aka 'Love Hurts') fame. We spent a memorable night in pubs waiting for the first train back to Genk. *Up the irons! Zap Stan*

Maiden raids Kortrijk

In 1980, Iron Maiden played their very first European gig in Kortrijk, Belgium. McKitty, the band I was drumming for, supported them at that gig. When our guitarist's amp broke down, I improvised a drum and bass guitar solo. According to Steve Harris, it was one of the best solos he had ever seen. Later, when drummer Clive left Maiden, I was the first replacement Steve called. I happened to be in the right place at the right time.
Nicko McBrain, Iron Maiden

© Jan Goedefroit

Nick was drumming for McKitty at the time; he was sitting outside a local café, dressed in a white suit, a Panama hat and pointy shoes. Because of his outfit, I thought he was a pimp or something. He had obviously had a few drinks and was chatting socially, and I thought, 'Whoah, who is this guy?' During the show, McKitty's guitar broke down halfway through the set. Nick ended up doing a solo of sorts while the rest tried to fix the guitar. Normally I find drum solos utterly boring, but this was more interesting than the rest of the set. He was great! *Steve Harris, Iron Maiden, based on the book 'Eddie Made Me Do It'*

© Archive Eric Deroo

During their show at the Maeke-Blyde on 11 October 1980, UK band Girl-school demolished the 'pussycat rock' tag once and for all. The band had just scored a modest hit with 'Demolition Boys', a song that deserved a more fitting title, like... 'Demolition Girls'.

Girlschool

Maeke-Blyde - Poperinge

11-10-1980

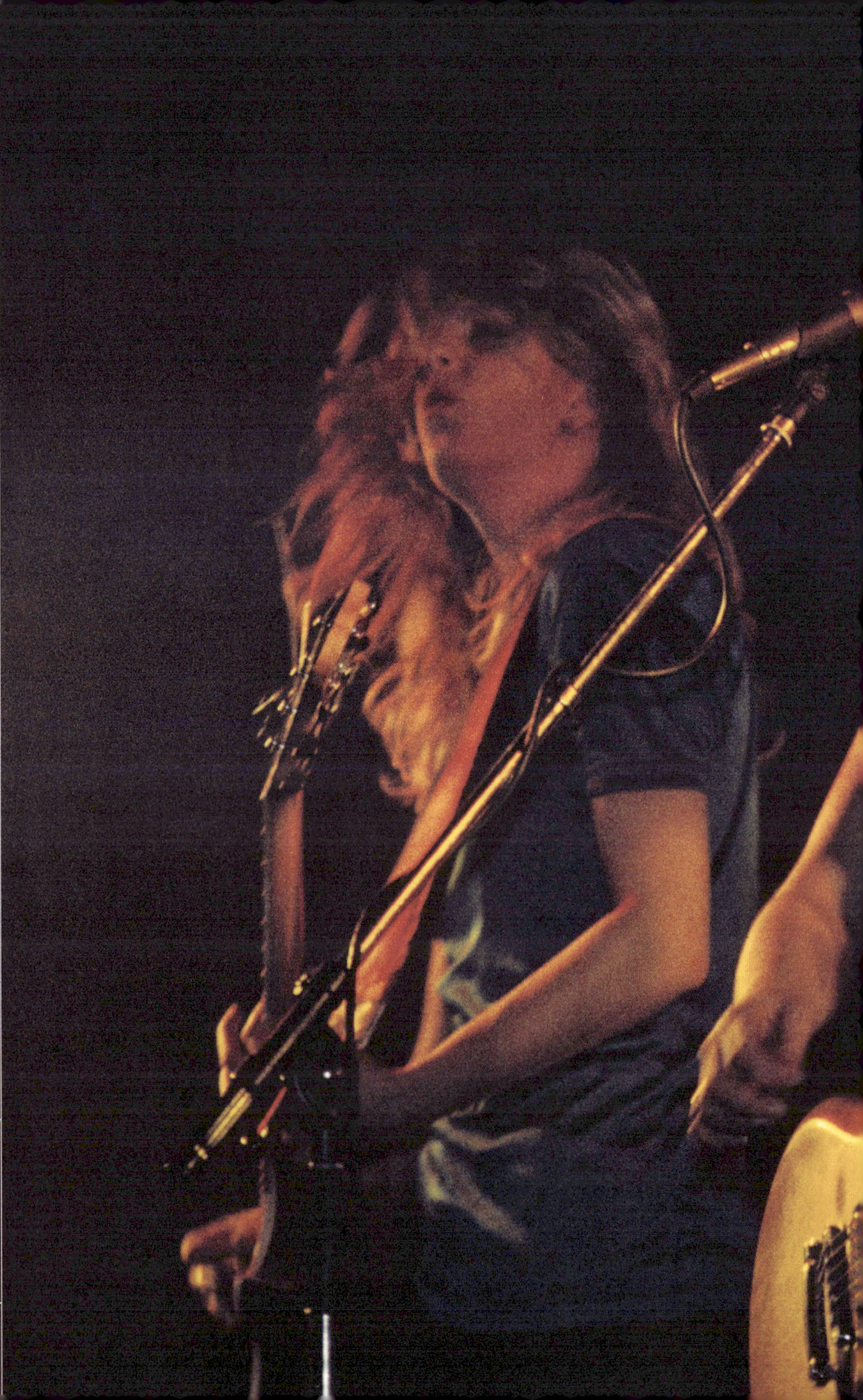

✝✝✝✝✝✝✝✝✝✝✝✝✝

The band played hard,
it played so loud.
The roof came crashing to
the ground. Demolition!

✝✝✝✝✝✝✝✝✝✝✝✝✝

© Archive Eric Deroo

Toet peist. Fresh like toothpaste.

In the late 1970s, I formed the band Tooth-Paste with guitarist Dominique Ryckaert from Menen. The name was deliberately made up of two words to sound as fresh as toothpaste. It's a play on the West Flemish expression 'Toet, peist!' - pronounced 'toothpaste' - which means 'yes, I think so!' Back then there were far fewer bands and social media didn't exist, so our live reputation was all we had. And it was excellent. The Flemish-Walloon language border was no barrier either. We were 'big in Mouscron and Comines', but we were also warmly welcomed in West Flanders.

My brother Bernard, who played both bass and guitar, was a child of the sixties and had a taste for prog rock (Yes, Camel and their ilk) and classic hard rock (The Who, Deep Purple and Led Zeppelin). Dominique Ryckaert, our Gibson-wielding guitarist, liked it a bit rougher (Ted Nugent, Accept and Molly Hatchet). Our drummer Jimmy Wyseur was a die-hard new waver. I absorbed and digested all of the above, but my musical world changed forever when the Sex Pistols shook the world with 'Never Mind

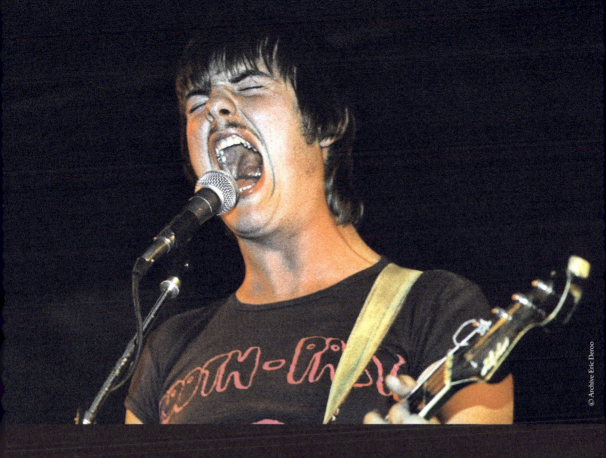

'The Bollocks' in 1976. This mishmash of styles prevented Tooth-Paste from being pigeonholed. Eventually, that led to our downfall. After the release of 'Just a Game' in 1982, our first (and last) single, things went downhill fast. The poppy tune wasn't representative of what Tooth-Paste was really about. So that's where it ended.

Anyway, in 1980 we supported Girlschool at the Maeke-Blyde. What should have been a highlight turned into an utter nightmare. Girlschool's engineer asked us if he could try out his brand new echo chamber during our show. Being the naive nineteen-year-old newbie that I was, I agreed. The result was that vocal lines from two songs earlier in our set reverberated through the speakers. Much to my surprise, this struck a chord with the audience. But after our show I stormed into the Girlschool dressing room to complain, burning with anger. I was met with irritated looks from four young ladies, two of whom were topless. All I could manage was a sheepish '*Oops, sorryhhh...*'. How's that for a sad beginning of the end? *Luc Dufourmont*

Beurshalle - Brugge

Golden Earring

✝✝✝✝✝✝✝✝✝✝✝✝✝

Our first 'big' concert
with Abasti drew
just over 2,000
visitors. Even Herman
Schueremans came to
check if we were any
good at organising
events like these. We
passed the litmus test
with flying colours and
many more events in
Poperinge followed.
But that Golden
Earring gig really was
our acid test!

Luc Weyaert

✝✝✝✝✝✝✝✝✝✝✝✝✝

Maeke-Blyde - Poperinge

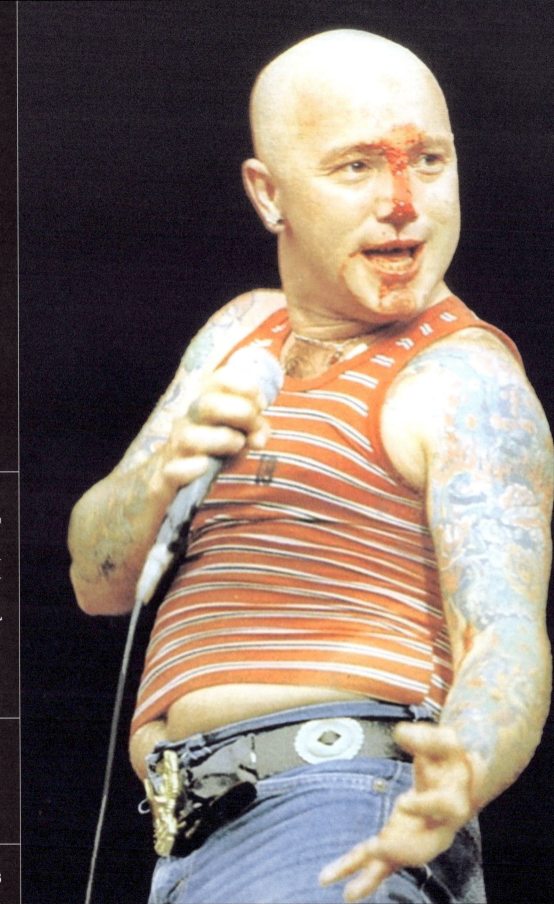

☩☩☩☩☩☩☩☩☩☩☩☩☩

I remember Rose Tattoo's very
short set. After only a few songs
it was 'game over'. Singer Angry
Anderson kept hitting himself in the
forehead with the microphone until
he passed out. The whole band were
also drunk as skunks, which was a
huge disappointment to me.

Filip Fieu

☩☩☩☩☩☩☩☩☩☩☩☩☩

'Nice boys don't play rock 'n' roll':
Rose Tattoo singer Angry Anderson
unleashing blood and thunder at the
Reading Festival in 1981. Unfortunately,
we haven't been able to dig up any
photos of his antics in Poperinge.

Tygers touring on the edge

After we signed with MCA in 1979, budget management became extremely strict. This led to us sleeping in modest accommodation on tour, often in the cheapest hotels. In March 1982, on a European tour through picturesque Belgium, we arrived, without the aid of modern navigation equipment, at a run-down property booked as a 'hotel' by our manager.

When we got there, this young woman in a nurse's getup welcomed us, which kind of hinted at the vibe. The whole place had this strange feel, you know, from the sterile smell to the hospital-style decor in our rooms. We were a bit puzzled but found it funny. I can still picture us hanging out in the bar, cracking up while this old bloke played pool and let out farts, non-stop. It was hilarious.

And that's what it smelled like on our tour bus. All the time. It may sound funny, but it soon became a source of irritation. Little food, little sleep and a lot of booze led to a lot of bickering between band and crew. Fatigue and hangovers sometimes led to less than perfect sets and eventually to line-up changes. But I think it's on the road that you really learn to be a band, not in a rehearsal room. *Robb Weir, Tygers of Pan Tang*

↓↓↓↓↓↓↓↓↓↓↓↓↓

Herman Schueremans, to whom we introduced Tygers of Pan Tang, didn't have a proper agreement with us. Normally we'd strike a fifty-fifty deal with him, sharing the costs and the profits equally. This time, however, he had his doubts about the whole thing and only contributed 15% of the costs (so he would only get 15% of the proceeds). In the end, 1,789 paying visitors came to the Maeke-Blyde, the largest number ever. When he realised how successful the show had been, he threatened that we'd never book another band through him again unless we coughed up another 50,000 Belgian francs (about 1,250 euros). We paid up to keep the peace. *Luc Waeyaert*

Venom   Maeke-Blyde - Poperinge

Venom played a series of chaotic gigs in old church halls, which made for juicy tales among the locals. Somehow this news travelled across the pond and the band got the chance to play a show at a Belgian sports hall called Maeke-Blyde. Venom wanted to break out of the UK, so they jumped at the chance. The show on 4 June 1982 was attended by over 3,000 fans. After this successful gig in Poperinge, the band set their sights on the States, which they took by storm. *Eric Cook, Venom manager*

I first met Eric Cook when I was about 16 years old. For our first Belgian gig in Poperinge, I asked him to be our guitar roadie. He later became our manager and almost everything we achieved after that was thanks to him. We were business partners and saw each other almost every day for twenty years. He was a fun guy to hang out with, but really determined when it came to business. He managed to do great things on a shoestring budget. Okay, we didn't always agree... but he always listened and was persuasive when the situation called for it. *Anthony 'Abaddon' Bray, Venom*

Metallica's first gig as a support act in Belgium was a close call. It almost fell through. The band's tour manager didn't trust our stage construction, he thought it was too unstable for their heavy lighting rigs. To quote his words: "*I don't care. Even if the fucking Beatles had played on it, we're not getting up on that stage.*" In desperation, I went through my contact list and called Noël Steen of Rock Torhout, one of the most renowned stage builders in the scene. With his expertise, he was in a much better position to negotiate with the rigid tour manager. In the end, everything fell into place. Even then Metallica was much better than Venom. Everyone just felt that they would soon become a metallic force to be reckoned with. *Jean-Pierre Staelen*

'Louder than Motörhead.' That's what it said on the sticky note next to that LP in the window of the Popcenter record shop. Was that even possible? The album came in a black sleeve with a golden Baphomet goat's head in a pentagram: 'Welcome to Hell' by Venom. I just had to listen to that ominous slab of vinyl. For me, Venom opened the infernal gates to the era of thrash, death and black metal. It was early 1980 and I was barely 15. My parents would never have allowed such sacrilege. But when my best mate won two tickets on a local radio station, I had to go. Venom in Poperinge, I was there... my first show ever! *Nolf Kaka*

HOME TAPING IS

KILLING MUSIC

SO ARE

A full concept:
the venom is in the tail

Raw songs
If you like your rock hard, masculine and brimming with adrenaline, Venom
is for you. Chainsaw guitars, thunderous drums and werewolf vocals combine
to create a hard-as-nails sound unlike anything heard before. Their lyrics are
satanic, but often tongue in cheek. Unfortunately, a small group of Norwegian
dimwits took the demonic messages a bit too literally in the early 90s. Somehow they read them as a call for arson and murder. Venom's songs have that
recognisable groove and catchy choruses that set them apart from the sheer
endless stream of black metal bands they inspired.

Unheard vocals
Cronos' vocals ooze charisma, authority and confidence. Perfect for this kind
of in-your-face metal. Many of the students at the Metal Institute of Thrash,
where Venom taught, have singers who suck and whose lyrics are often unin-
telligible. That's not how I like my metal.

All-embracing image
Aesthetics and music have always been linked. In the beginning, Venom
invested a lot in their image. That's exactly what drew me to Venom's striking
album covers as a teenager. The logo, the unflinching lyrics and their over-
the-top attitude. It's no coincidence that Venom T-shirts are still bestsellers
today. Along with Motörhead's Snaggletooth and Maiden's Eddie, the Venom
goat is one of the most iconic heavy metal designs to date.

    I remember how many hard rockers and metalheads in my local pub
hated Venom. Some even called them punk. I saw them live for the first
time in 1982 in Poperinge. In 1984 I saw them again in the same place, this
time supported by a young Metallica. 'Welcome To Hell' and 'Black Metal'
are downright classics in my eyes. Pentagrams, candles and other satanic
imagery: visually Venom were way ahead of their time. They invented the
term black metal, and that's something a lot of self-proclaimed 'true black
metal' fans seem to forget. *Sam V*

I was at that Venom gig in Poperinge in 1982. And I still have the neck of the guitar that Mantas thrashed on stage. I got my original ticket signed by all three band members. After the gig, we went down to Bruges with the band to drink beer and raise hell. *Gunther Ranwez*

At one point we were offered the support slot on a Motörhead tour. It would have been a great opportunity for us, but in the end it didn't work out. I don't remember exactly why, but Tank got the job. A little later we accepted an invitation to play a show in Belgium with Picture and Acid. It was my first time outside the UK and there were about 3,000 people there.

   It was also the first time that Cronos handled the vocals. The three of us went, plus Eric Cook as a guitar roadie. He felt that Venom had the potential to go places and started making some phone calls. John Zazula from New York got us two gigs, so my second 'real' Venom gig ever was in NYC. *Anthony 'Abaddon' Bray, Venom*

We supported Venom at their very first show on the mainland, along with Picture. I remember setting up our gear in front of their huge drum kit. We were packed on stage like sardines! But the reaction of the crowd was overwhelming for us. It felt great because Venom played a different kind of metal, we just happened to sing about the same satanic themes. Anyway, thankfully they didn't realise that we were actually making fun of the whole thing while they seemed to take it so seriously. *Acid*

In the early 1980s, it was all the rage in metal circles to flirt with war and warfare. This ranged from Viking and Celtic symbolism to memorabilia from both World Wars. The American Confederate flag, known as the 'Southern Cross', was particularly popular. It often adorned shirts, patches and appeared in logos. This dark fascination seeped in via the biker culture. With its roots in American redneck culture, it was also eagerly adopted by members of the Ku Klux Klan. To put it mildly, it's a highly controversial symbol. Some say it represents blatant racism and nostalgia for slavery, while others see it simply as a symbol of Southern pride. For most of the metalheads in the Westhoek, the flag, with its fiery red and deep blue colours, was first and foremost just a 'cool symbol'. And apparently the organisers of Venom's 1982 show at the Maeke-Blyde were unaware of its historical connotations and significance. When the Newcastle band first saw the promo poster for the gig, they saw their band name backed by a confederate flag. Understandably, Venom were furious to be associated with a symbol of such dubious reference. It should come as no surprise that West Flanders was known as 'Texas' at the time.

KORTRIJK - Popcenter
OOSTENDE - Barbe-Q

DIKSMUIDE - 't Kabaretje
POPERINGE - Ons Huis -
Keikop - Hoppebel

ROESELARE - Klup
TORHOUT - Buffalo - Gipsy
- Melody Maker

bilbo brugge - gent

Picture

BRUG
GENT

BRUSSEL - Caroline Music
ANTWERPEN -
Brabo Records

LEUVEN - Campus
MECHELEN -
Center Fonoplaten

HASSELT - Hittip
CHARLEROI - Lido Music

20u VR.4
MAEKEBLIJD

LILLE · La Petite Cœur
AALTER · Music House

AALST · Solbemol
RONSE · Music Bar

WETTEREN · Music Machine
LOKEREN · Fonotheek

Pub · Bilbo

ACID

HEAVY SOUND

Presents

LIÈGE · Caroline Music
NAMUR · La Disquerie

V.V. HEAVY SOUND · BRUGGE
VRIJ VAN ZEGEL
(K.B. Art. 198/7)

UNI 1982
POPERINGE

VOORVERKOOP : 280 fr.
INGANG : 320 fr.

Zeefdruk STEEN   050.21.35.24

BTM concerts
i.s.m. FRITS HIRSCHLAND

Presenteert

KAZIMIERZ LUX

IN CONCERT

ZATERDAG 25 OKTOBER

ALAN. J. WALKER · ETIENNE VANNESTE   a KRIM PRODUCTION
presents

U.F.O.

PREMIER FOR BELGIUM

:MADE IN BELGIUM:

**DONDERDAG
JEUDI   15 NOVEMBRE 73**

HALLENns **KORTRIJK
COURTRAI**

**Met medewerking
PLAY-BOX Kuurne**

GWENDOLINE

ALAN J. WALKER · ETIENNE VANNESTE · KRIM PRODUCTION
Presents

**black
sabbath**

SUPPORTING ACT

**ZATERDAG
SAMEDI   12 JANUARI
VIER 74** TE 19H.
A

**HALLEN   KORTRIJK
HALLES   COURTRAI**

Met medewerking

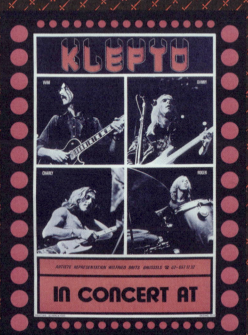

KLEPTO

WIM   DANNY

CHARLY   ROGER

ARTIESTE REPRESENTATION WILFRIED BAITS BRUSSELS ☎ 02-637 17 37

IN CONCERT AT

SPORTHAL KOEKELAERE
vrijdag 27 oktober te 20 u
V.Z.W. WOODLAND presenteert

AC/DC

VOORVERKOOP

BRUGGE: bilbo - hifihome - buffa music center
GENT: bilbo
KORTRIJK: popcenter
OOSTENDE: de beurs
TORHOUT: evergreen - de kelder
MALDEGEM: de walrus
ROESELARE: bilbo

ROCK POP JAZZ & BLUES
vrije ingang: opening zaterdag 28 oktober
RECORD SHOP
MELODY MAKER
PUTSTRAAT, 1 - TORHOUT

ver. utg. V.Z.W. WOODLAND zuidstr. torhout
zeefdruk DICTUS tel 66.95.48

MAEKEBLIJDE POPERINGE
ZATERDAG 25 APRIL 81 OM 20 UUR
SAMEDI AVRIL A HRS.

HARDROCK WITH

Rose Tattoo

+ SUPPORT

KAARTEN:
POPERINGE A La Fabrique, Ons Huis
IEPER San Marco
MENEN The Crimson

KORTRIJK Popcenter
KOEKELARE 't Schrijvertjs
HANDZAME De Meeuwe
TIELT DeMarbel

ROESELARE Piet Gein
BRUGGE Bilbo
DIKSMUIDE 't Kabaretje
TORHOUT Melody Maker

VRIJ VAN ZEGEL CULT. DOEL
Zeefdruk Steen oso.11 35 24

MAEKEBLIJDE POPERINGEN
(DOORNSTRAAT)
VRIJDAG VENDREDI 18 MEI MAI 20 HRS UUR
LION CONCERTS NV. i.a.w. ODIL CONCERTS PRESENTS

RUSH

+MAX WEBSTER BAND

POPERINGEN: à la Fabrique Handelsbeurs
IEPER: Van 't sevenant
MENEN: Disco Bar
KORTRIJK: Pop Center
LILLE: Paris Music
ROESELARE: Piet Gein
ARMENTIER: Penez
MOUSCRON: Le Top
TIELT: Dzjing's
GENT: Bilbo Music Man
BRUGGE: Bilbo Pols Music Center
TORHOUT: Melody Maker
VEURNE: Muziek Doos

zeefdruk DICTUS tel 66.95.48

Alan.J.Walker.de KRIMSON, ... presents:

SAMEDI 29 Septembre à 19h.

hawkwind
Fruup & Andy Dunkley
DISC·JOCKEY

billets :
PREVENTE
hawkwind & chicken-shack
(20 sept.) à 14 et à 20) 2£

à l'entrée
hawkwind 18
chicken-shack 12 h.

reservations:
· GWENDOLINE
5 rue Nicolas Leblanc LILLE
tel. 54 61 29
· MAISON SCREPEL-POLLET
rer Carrière
138 Grande Rue ROUBAIX

halles·COURTRAI

GULLEGEM: LAS PA

OUDEJAARSFUIF 31 DECEMBER OM 21 UUR
MET OPTREDEN VAN

T R A N C E

INKOM: 500 F.

PRIJES, OFZE VERDESSORU KREAGRAPEK · GULLEGEM · TEL. 056/41.82.75

LION CONCERTS nv
i.a.w. ODIL CONCERTS presents

Rush -|- Max Webster Band

Vrijdag 18 mei 1979 - 20 uur
Vendredi 18 mai 1979 - 20 h

MAEKEBLIJDE - Doornstraat
P O P E R I N G E

250 Fr.   ⎡00026

TAKSEN EN B.T.W. INBEGREPEN
Te tonen op aanvraag - Niet geldig z. strook
TAXES ET TVA COMPRISES
A présenter s. dem. - Non valable s. souche

TICKETS VOET - 9800 DEINZE

'maeckeblyde' poperinge

zaterdag 25 april 1981 om 20.00 uur

se tattoo + SUPPORT ACT

fr.   № 0286

LION CONCERTS nv
i.a.w. ODIL CONCERTS presents

Rush -|- Max Webster Band

Vrijdag 18 mei 1979   20 uur
Vendredi 18 mai 1979   20 h

MAEKEBLIJDE - Doornstraat
P O P E R I N G E

220 Fr.   00288

TAKSEN EN B.T.W. INBEGREPEN
Te tonen op aanvraag - Niet geldig z. strook
TAXES ET TVA COMPRISES
A présenter s. dem. - Non valable s. souche

TICKETS VOET - 9800 DEINZE

Zaal BELFORT - Poperinge

ODIL-CONCERTS presents

GIRLSSCHOOL

Zaterdag 11 oktober 1980 te 20.30 u.

200 Fr.

00162

TAKSEN EN BTW INBEGREPEN
Te tonen op aanvraag - Niet geldig z. strook
TICKETS VOET - 9800 DEINZE

Brugge - Beurshalle

Vrijdag 24 september 1982 te 20.00 u.

RAVEN
ACCEPT

supportact : Crossfire

All glass containers, cans firecrackers, fireworks, recorders and cameras excepting small
instamatic type cameras are strictly prohibited
in the hall and can be seized by artist
management and/or concert promotors.

V.V. : 300

ING. : 350   № 02037

KOEKELARE (B.) - ZUUDHOVE
Vrijdag 11 november '83 - 20 u.
Vendredi 11 Novembre '83 - 20 h.

Budgie Trance

Voorverkoop: 200 Fr.   Kassa: 200 Fr.
Prevente: 45 Fr.   Caisse: 50 FF.

pvba Brouwerij LOOTENS
Ringlaan 87 - 8280 KOEKELARE

№ 4037

MEKADO HARD-ROCK
CONSERT '82

Brugge Beurshalle
9 april '82 - 20 u. 30

ACID
BODINE
ACCEPT

All glass containers, cans, firecrackers, fireworks, recorders and cameras excepting small
instamatic type cameras are strictly prohibited
in the hall and can be seized by artist
management and/or concert promotors.

280 F   320 F
V.V.   ING.

TICKETS VOET - 9800 DEINZE   00757

DONDERDAG 4 MEI 1978

te 20.30 uur

VAN HALEN

ZAAL MAEKE BLYDE - POPERINGE

VOORVERKOOP : 190 fr.

448   AAN DE KASSA : 220 fr.

★ KAYAK ★
★ KAZIMIR LUX ★
koekelare   **18 okt 1975**

voor uw muziekinstrumenten
MUSIC EXPRESS
noordstr. 148 roeselare   tel 051·20 06 19

---

saturday 11 september 1976 20 h.

TED NUGENT
+ support act.

Ontmoetingscentrum
HARELBEKE

220 Fr.

№ - 00049

TAKSEN EN B.T.W. INBEGREPEN
Te tonen op aanvraag · Niet geldig zonder strook

TICKETS VOET — 9800 DEINZE

ALAN J. WALKER - ETIENNE VANNESTE

presents a KRIM production

U. F. O.
Premier for Belgium.

— MADE IN BELGIUM —

15 november 1973

HALLEN KORTRIJK

№ 1003

België prijs : 120 fr.
France prix : 15 F.

RORY GALLAGHER
CONCERT

DE HALLEN
KORTRIJK   COURTRAI

Woensdag 16 oktober 1974, 20 uur
Mercredi 16 octobre 1974, 20 h.

150 Fr.

№ 00381

ORG. : De Hoop - Waregem
De Stovepijs - Kortrijk

TICKETS VOET — 9800 DEINZE

Lion promotions i.a.w.
Metropolitan entertainment
presents

the electronic magic of
TANGERINE DREAM
Ontmoetingscentrum HARELBEKE
Donderdag 18 nov. te 20 h 30

220 Fr.   01840

TAKSEN EN B.T.W. INBEGREPEN
Te tonen op aanvraag · Niet geldig zonder strook

TICKETS VOET — 9800 DEINZE

Beurshalle - Brugge

zaterdag
18 oktober 1980
20 uur

ABASTI - concerts vzw presents

JARDON LANE · ONCE MORE
GOLDEN EARRING

Voorverkoop : 230 fr.
№   686   Deuren : 280 fr.

KISS
+ SUPPORTING ACT

Ontmoetingscentrum
Bij het station   Près de la gare
HARELBEKE
op 3 km van Kortrijk   à 3 km de Courtrai

Zondag 6 juni 1976 om 20 h
Dimanche 6 juin 1976 à 20 h

220 BF

PAUL
STANLEY

A présenter sur demande
Te tonen op aanvraag · Niet geldig zonder

Tickets VOET – Deinze

PW

ODIL CONCERTS I.S.M. LION PROMOTION
PRESENTEREN

ZONDAG 4 DECEMBER

te 20.30 uur

THE RUNAWAY

MAEKE BLYDE - POPERIN

№ 166   INKOM 180 F.

Maeck blyde - Poperinge
Vrijdag 4 juni 1982 te 20u00
Vendredi 4 juin 1982 à 20h00

Venom
Picture Acid

All glass bottles, cans, firecrackers, fireworks, radios and cameras excepting small instamatic type cameras are strictly prohibited in the hall. This can be seized by artist management and concert promoters.

V.V.-A.V. 280
ENTREE 320 F   № 0328

MAECKEBLYDE POPERINGE VRIJDAG/VENDREDI 29 JAN. 82, 20 uh

New Abasti Concerts presenteert

GILLAN
TYGERS OF PAN TANG

Zeefdruk Steen 050.21.35.24

VRIJ VAN ZEGEL CULT. DOEL.

TICKETS:
OOSTENDE Barbe Q
WETTEREN Music Machine
MEULEBEKE Onderkomen
MOUSKRON Skyline
GENT Music Man Bilbo
OUDENAARDE Brouwershuis
AALST Salbemol DENZE Wave
GERAARDSBERGEN Floeren
VLAMERTINGE Barroa
BRUGGE Bilbo

DIKSMUIDE 'Kabaretje
TIELT Marbel
HANDZAME De Meeuw
KORTEMARK Sing Song
DEERLIJK 't Haantie
POPERINGE Kekop Hopperbel
Ons Huis

IZEGEM De Sterre
MENEN De Krinson
DENDERMONDE Solbemol
KORTRIJK Popcenter
TORHOUT Melody Maker
ROESELARE Piet Gein Klap
IEPER Hoppy Days
WERVIK Klup
LILLE Music Hallen
La Petito Coeur

KOEKELARE JEUGDKROEG SKOE BIDOE

KLUP
OOSTSTR. ROES.
NIEUWSTR. WERV.

KLUP de platenzaak voor poplefhebbers

MAEKEBLIJDE POPERINGE VRIJDAG/VENDREDI 21 MAART/MARS

LION CONCERTS i.a.w. ODIL CONCERTS present

20,30u

in CONCERT

motörhead

BOMBER TOUR '80

TICKETS
POPERINGE a la fabrique
Jongheerd Ghylin
platenhandel Hopperbel
Zwembad De Couter
VLAMERTINGE Barroo
MENEN Discobar

IEPER Vonnerboum
KORTRIJK Phpcenter
MOUSKRON Le Toys
BRUGGE Bilbo
Poply Revue center
ROESELARE Piet Gein

ARMENTIERE Penez
LILLE Le Froic
DIKSMUIDE Musick Expres
TIELT Dixis
TORHOUT Melody Maker

ZEEFDRUK STEEN 060-213524

MEKADO HARD-ROCK CONCERT '82

BRUGGE BEURSHALLE

VRIJDAG 9 APRIL 20U00

ACID
BODINE
ACCEPT

INLICHTINGEN (050) 200576 voorverkoop 28?-f

BELFORT POPERINGE

zaterdag 11 oktober - 20u30

ODIL CONCERTS PRESENTS

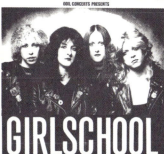

GIRLSCHOOL

TICKETS:
POPERINGE: A la Fabrique   IEPER: Happy Days   KORTRIJK: Popcenter
   Platen Hoppebel   MENEN: Diskobar   ROESELARE: Piet Gein
   Jeugdheem   Jan de Lichte   LILLE: le Fnac
VLAMERTINGE: Barroo   Krimson   TORHOUT: Melody Maker

Zeefdruk STEEN 050/21 35 24

ZATERDAG 18 OKTOBER
BRUGGE BEURSHALLE

ABASTI CONCERTS VZW PRESENTEERT

JARDON LANE
ONCE MORE
Golden Earring

VOORVERKOOP : 230 FR.

KASSA : 290 FR.

Tickets :

OOSTENDE : Bar B.Q.   MALDEGEM : Wielux
AALTER : Luxor (bij the Manden)   BRUGGE : Beho
ROESELARE : Piet Gein : T.Kartiershop
VEURNE : Boulevarder   GENT : Music Man
DIKSMUIDE : Katshuisle   WAREGEM : De Hoop
TORHOUT : Melody Maker   GISTEL : Jürgen Tienjes
KOEKELARE : Schooimke   IEPER : San Mario
RUMBEKE : Til   KORTRIJK : Popcenter
KORTEMARK : Sino Sino

Druk Davidse Handsome.

Koekelare (B) - Zuudhove

Vrijdag 11 nov. 83 - 20 u.
Vendredi 11 nov. 83 - 20 h.

BUDGIE
TRANCE

INFO : 2e HEAVY SOUND FESTIVAL : BRUGGE
zond. 10 juni 84   dim. 10 juni 84

TICKETS
ANTWERPEN : De Zaro   LOFTENAUDE : T.Schild
BRUGGE : Billiartkel   MEUWPOORT : Blikn' Bar
DIKSMUIDE : Friesken Fub   OOSTENDE : Berlin V
DIKSMUIDE : Levendekol   OOSTENDE : Platenjeshop
GENT : Billu   POPERINGE : Ons Huis
GENT : Music Man   ROESELARE : Ad Fundum
GISTEL : Banel Pub   ROESELARE : Piet Gein
HOUTHULST : Kontuuri   STADEN : Specman
IEPER : Happy Days   TORHOUT : Mart
IZEGEM : J.F Ring   VEURNE : The Cricket
KOEKELARE : Skoebidoe   VEURNE : Festuum
KORTEMARK : Sing Sing   ZONNEBEKE (P), Di. O. Neuma. et Va.
KORTRIJK : Popcenter   LILLE: Fnanc

Fonoplaten en popkledij
Happy Days
Ieper - De Panne

Jeugdkroeg Skoebidoe
Bij Dirk & Myranda
Oostmeetstraat 6 - Koekelare

MAEKE BLYDE - POPERINGE (Blg)

ODIL CONCERTS PRESENTS

VAN
HALEN

DONDERDAG 4 MEI '78 TE 20.30 u.

RESERVATIONS :

Poperinge : A la fabrique Tel. 057 33 30 86
Ieper : Ramevensant Tel 057 20 08 48
Kortrijk : Popcenter Tel 056 21 94 89
Roeselare : Piet Hein

Lille : Paris Musique Tel. 20 57 46 01
Brugge : Bilbo Tel. 050 33 40 11
Paul's Music Center Tel. 050 33 56 24
Gent : Bilbo Tel. 091 22 63 65
Tielt : Brimm'

ZAAL MAEKEBLIJDE POPERINGE

ODIL CONCERTS presents:

THE
RUNAWAYS

ZONDAG   **4 DECEMB**ere   TE
DIMANCHE   re   A   **20H30**

reservations:

the Belgian fab four

With a metallic storm of riffs sweeping over the Flemish fields, it doesn't take long for rehearsal rooms to spring up in back rooms, stables, garden sheds and above local cafés. And soon, we proved to be masters of our craft. A rich metal scene began to bloom in an almost endless number of metal pubs, youth clubs and green meadows. Those who take the time to listen to this early incarnation of Belgian metal today cannot help but be in awe. Acid, Crossfire, Killer and Ostrogoth, the four torchbearers of that era, still amaze us with their unadulterated brand of heavy metal. Other bands such as Purple Haze, Bad Lizard, Buzzard, Lions Pride, Thunderfire and Treason joined the ranks. Not much later, armed and ready youngsters like Cyclone and Target followed in the footsteps of their predecessors.

A tsunami floods West Flanders

Somewhere at the intersection of the dark seventies and the glitter of the eighties, the New Wave Of British Heavy Metal – NWOBHM in short – swept the world. The tidal wave rolled in from the other side of the Channel, from Britain's rough working-class neighbourhoods. But unlike the socially critical aspect of punk, this new school of heavy metal was all about claiming your personal freedom. The genre's non-conformist stance appealed to a wider audience, from bearded bikers to long-haired outcasts. Punk, on the other hand, with its ideological bent, was particularly popular among students. Metal was often dismissed as its 'dumber little brother'. But listen carefully and you will hear the musical and melodic craftsmanship that most punk lacked. And in retrospect, it's striking how artificial the dividing line between the two genres actually was, and still is. Battalions of fresh metal soldiers with a DIY attitude borrowed from punk came ashore in West Flanders: Iron Maiden, Saxon, Tygers of Pan Tang and an army of others conquer our stages and take no prisoners. They turned a tenacious work ethic into an art, stubbornly swimming against the tide. The up-and-coming NWOBHM bands are brimming with passion and sheer enthusiasm. Blistering riffs. Rhythm sections to build upon. Tight musicianship topped by twin guitar solos. In short: stuff that makes you want to break out the air guitar and go wild.

New bands are formed in the many metal pubs that spring up in the region. Flemings are proving to be very adept at their own version of this new brand of metal. And the sturdy West Flemish soil seems to be an ideal breeding ground. It is teeming

↓↓↓↓↓↓↓↓↓↓↓↓↓

A vibrant scene is taking shape, spearheaded by the so-called Fab Four of Flemish metal: Acid, Crossfire, Killer and Ostrogoth.

↓↓↓↓↓↓↓↓↓↓↓↓↓

with devout Catholics, but without the fundamentalism of the Bible Belt. So there is plenty to rebel against without too much resistance. We indulge in the absurdity of 'pseudo' Satanism as if it were a heavy Trappist beer. Sometimes it feels as if we were thrown into a magic cauldron boiling with sarcasm at birth. A shabby bar with bearded bikers would occasionally get a frown or a scowl from the congregation, but they weren't entirely condemned either. Meanwhile, in the shadows of West Flanders, the demons of metal continue to blow minds and claim souls. A vibrant scene is taking shape, spearheaded by the so-called Fab Four of Flemish metal: Acid, Crossfire, Killer and Ostrogoth. Add a dash of Bad Lizard and you have a highly flammable cocktail.

Grassroots metal

Pubs all over West Flanders were transformed into metal havens. One of them, Den Tunnel café in Kortrijk, was a pub where people played cards on weekdays, and a metal bar at weekends. Every Friday, metal posters were meticulously pinned up, and taken down again every Monday morning. Metal hotspots could be identified by the rows of heavy motorbikes parked outside. The printed press also played its part. The teen magazine Joepie had its weekly 'Betonmolen'* column, filled with interviews, reviews and gig announcements. But even more important were the many fantastic fanzines. These handmade masterpieces praised our beloved metal bands. Xeroxed in small quantities and distributed locally, they advertised local releases and announced shows in Belgium and abroad. The Dutch magazine 'Aardschok' deserves special mention: it was later professionalised and is still in print today.

* Flemish, translates as 'concrete mixer'

In the previous chapter, the actions of Jacques Merlevede of the Popcenter in Kortrijk proved how strong the impact of a local record shop could be. But it wasn't just about sales. The importance of the Belgian record label Mausoleum should not be underestimated. The label not only provided a launching pad for local releases, it soon became a household name in the European hard rock and metal scene and beyond: Anvil, Hawkwind, Voïvod, Warlock,... their artist portfolio was truly impressive. In the end, however, Mausoleum didn't survive its legal and financial problems, which led to the pre-mature burial of releases, such as Killer's planned live album.

Bring in a sociologist and he will praise the *bottom-up, grassroots approach* of the metal scene in our Flemish fields. But who needs buzzwords, right? Anyone who was there will tell you that there was definitely metal in the West Flemish tap water back then. Today, general pop culture is permeated by metal bands and their iconography - Metallica shirts at H&M, anyone? - but we sometimes seem to forget how important our home-grown bands were in the history of heavy metal. High time we put together four tributes, one for each of our Fab Four.

Acid: the kids are Hooked on Metal

In the early 80s, the metal genre spread its tentacles even further. Motörhead provided the blueprint for speed metal with their high-octane brand of hard rock, and Venom paved the way for countless thrash metal and black metal bands. These two new styles would lead many kids down the left-hand path, including in Bruges, where the band Previous Page changed their name to Acid. Their trademark: breakneck riffs, screaming guitars, lots of double bass drums and the powerful voice of singer Kate. Their new formula would soon cause a serious stir among headbangers worldwide.

Singer Kate says, "I was one of the first women to front a metal band. That meant you had to prove yourself more. And that hasn't changed. First they judge you by your looks. Then, if you're lucky, they look at how talented or creative you are. There was also some jealousy from more established bands. We were newcomers and we got picked up almost immediately, while they had been around for a long time. And that stung."

"I grew up among bikers. I had a moped myself and later I got a Yamaha 650cc bike. Most bikers like rough music, but we hardly realised that what we were playing was heavy metal. We were young and didn't really give it that much thought. Being creative, doing it all ourselves with a positive attitude, that's what motivated us. We just wanted to have fun and enjoy ourselves. And yeah, we got lucky. 'Hooked On Metal', our first 7", sounded so awful that we decided to keep the pressing limited. I think our shoestring budget somehow determined the quality of that single. Much to our surprise, fans of more extreme metal around the world snapped up the record. So I guess our energy caught on after all."

International box office success

Luc Van den Bossche - the owner of the Bilbo record shop in Bruges, where the band often hung out – rustled up a shady record deal with Mausoleum Records. Drummer Geert 'Anvill' recalls: "He demanded that we sell the rights to our music. But that was a bridge too far for us, so we decided to release our debut LP ourselves."

On 'Maniac', Acid's second album, the band nails all the metal clichés. The sound is fast and furious. You'll get the picture when you hear what four-legged drummer Anvill is doing on the track 'Bottoms Up'. And so Acid find themselves in the cradle of speed metal without even realising it. 'Maniac' sold more than 19,000 copies, which makes it a real blockbuster for a local band in a niche genre. According to stories from the time, Luc literally wallpapered his Bilbo record shop with the album.

Acid

© Frederick Moulaert

Lyrically the group is often pigeonholed. Geert 'Anvill': "We were not so much about devilry and all that. Thematically I think we were more about the freedom of riding around on motorbikes. The whole lifestyle that goes with it, you know. For me, Acid was a lot more Motörhead and less Venom. It was all moving so fast, new sub-genres in metal were almost impossible to follow. In the late 80s metal became more extreme, faster and more brutal. Although we were musically at our best on our third full-length album 'Engine Beast', it was to be our last release. In a way we had been beaten at our own game by the competition. But we never followed trends, it just wasn't in our nature to copy those bands."

As they say, it's better to burn out than to fade away. Acid had their brief *moment de gloire* and left us three great albums that are still highly sought after by lovers of fierce metal. Many fans have taken them to their hearts and remain loyal to this day.

I still listen to Acid. They were larger than life and revolutionary. As far as I know, they were the first speed metal band in the world with a front woman. And they played faster than anyone else around these parts. As Bruges was their home base, they had hordes of die-hard fans there, which is typical for West Flanders. Many West Flemish towns had their own hard rock pub where biker gangs would hang out. On Saturday nights we would go from bar to bar, starting fights with the disco crowd and basically anyone who got in our way. Sometimes the situation would turn around and we would get our arses kicked. Or we'd get picked up by the cops. I've also seen some pretty rough scenes at gigs, especially when rival biker gangs clashed. It was a bit like the Wild West back then. *Peter V.*

In Joepie #463 we read something in the 'Oorspijs' section that pissed us off. The review of the new album by Bruges heavy metal band Acid stated that the band wasn't mature enough to release an album yet. We disagree! The proof of their maturity and success is clear: within the first week of its release, they already sold 2,000 copies. Acid have been asked to support big names like Motörhead, Viva and Killer, so how's that for a quality check? Our advice: go and see the band live before you spew your critique. You'll have to agree that Acid are a rock solid band. *Nathalie Aelens and Ann Cooremans (Anti-review in Joepie magazine)*

BRUGGE - SCHUTTERSHOF
VRIJDAG 24 JUNI '83 20.30u

ACID

Zaterdag 21 April 1984
Schuttershof St.Kruis Brugge
M.C.BIKE RIDERS ORGANISEERT
HARD & HEAVY

ACID
BAD LIZARD

AANVANG 20U.   VOORVERKOOP 150   DEUREN 180

M.C. BIKE RIDERS

CAFE DRIVE INN
LOKAAL BIKE RIDERS
GISTELSESTEENWEG 22

MUZIEK VOOR IEDEREEN

VOORVERKOOP
DRIVE INN   GISTELSE STEENWEG
PIN-UP   LANGESTRAAT
BILBO   NOORDZANDSTRAAT
TVINKSKE   LANGE REI
SCHUTTERSHOF   BOOGSCHUTTERSLAAN

MIDDELKERKE - Zaal TER DUINEN
OP ZATERDAG 3 APRIL 1982

JAARLIJKS FANBAL VAN

disco IMAGICO

en met het optreden van de

rockgroep ACID

Voorverkoop : 100 Fr.   Zaal : 120 Fr.

Vrije Radio Blankenberge   FM 100.7 Mhz
Woensdag 11 augustus 1982
In tent te Wenduine - De Haan

BELGIAN HEAVY-METAL CONCERT

Purple Haze   Ostrogth
Stainless Steel   Acid

Zeilen open : 18.30 u.   Inkom : 299
Aanvang : ± 19.15 u.   Voorverkoop : 299
IEDEREEN IS VAN HARTE WEL...

BRUGGE - SINT-KRUIS   -   SCHUTTERSHOF
VRIJDAG 24 JUNI 1983 te 20.30 uur

ACID

Voorverkoop: 120 F

Kassa: 150 F

Taksen en BTW inbegrepen

De inrichter is niet verantwoordelijk
voor gebeurlijke ongevallen of schade.   N°

SINT-KRUIS BRUGGE SCHUTTERSHOF

VRIJDAG 24 JUNI OM 20.30 UUR.

BRUGGE'S HEAVY'METAL BAND

acid

IN CONCERT

IF YOU'RE HOOKED ON METAL

YOU JUST HAVE TO BE THERE

---

zat. 14 nov. '81
zaal tramhuis
Assebroek
optreden: ACID
+ party met tnt
aanv. 20.30 u

PIERRE DE GRANDE presenteert

ACID + KILLER

ZATERDAG 23 OCTOBER 1982 - 20 u.
ZATERDAG 23 OCTOBER 1982 - 20 u.
Zaal ZUIDHOVE - KOEKELARE
Vooraf : 150,-   Deur : 180,-

STAD GISTEL   —   SPORTHAL

Zaterdag 28 augustus 1982 vanaf 19u30' :

Rock Fuif met

B.O.G. en «ACID»

en Radio Rock Torhout's Drive In Show.

VOORVERKOOP : 130 F. — AAN DE DEUR : 150 F.

PIERRE DE GRANDE PRESENTEERT

ACID KILLER

Zat. 23 Oktober '82 - 20u.
ZUUDHOVE KOEKELARE

VOOR : 150 F.   **DEUR : 180 F.**

TICKETS
KOEKELARE: Scooby Doo, Sing Song, Non Stop Music Center-
MOERE: Jeugdforum - KORTEMARK: Sing Song -
BRUGGE: Bilbo - GISTEL: The Barrel Pub - TORHOUT: Gipsy,
Buffalo - OOSTENDE: Centerfold, Barbe Q -
BLANKENBERGE: Cadillac

NON STOP MUSIC CENTER
Sterrestraat 58 Koekelare
051/58.99.44

Zeefdruk Steen 050.21 35 24

Zaterdag 21 April 84
Schuttershof St.Kruis Brugge
M.C. BIKE RIDERS Organiseert
HARD & HEAVY

ACID
BAD LIZARD

Aanvang 20u   Voorverkoop 150   Deuren 180

Crossfire: See you in hell

Crossfire was born from the remnants of the punk band The Onion Dolls. As the New Wave Of British Heavy Metal washed over Europe, Crossfire got hooked too. They moved away from punk and bravely surfed the new metal wave.

Their sound was melodic and solid, with a distinctive rough edge. Vocalist Peter De Wint: "We wanted to be in a league of our own and I think we succeeded. The early days were a struggle. We used to rehearse frequently in my parents' hall in Nieuwerkerken and then go out and play until we dropped. We always rehearsed as if we were playing live and gave it our all. Hell yeah, we really rehearsed a lot."

The band's big break came in 1982 when Aardschock magazine included two of their songs on the 'Metal Clogs' compilation. Peter De Wint continues, "When we suddenly started getting gigs in the Netherlands, we felt that the band was really taking off. Not much later we signed a record deal with Mausoleum and the rest is history. We shared the bill with Ostrogoth quite a few times. Once I got a bike helmet thrown at my head by one of their 'rival' fans. I managed to dodge it by an inch ... The funny thing is: I later joined Ostrogoth as their lead singer.

In 1983, Crossfire released their first album on Mausoleum. 'See You in Hell' became an instant hit: melodic and energetic heavy metal with a touch of thrash. Fans raved and compared the band to Helloween and Accept. "We played at the third edition of Heavy Sound in Poperinge in 1985 and it's still a personal highlight. I never understood why the Belgian press always looked down on Crossfire. At one point we had the third best selling record in Belgium. We were asked to perform at the national Radio 2 Zomerhit in Blankenberge, but nobody mentioned that we sold more records than the big Belgian hit band De Kreuners. Only Flemish crooner Will Tura and comedian Urbanus outsold us that year!"

'Second Attack', the sophomore Crossfire album, was released in 1985. A third album was released in 1986. But 'Sharpshooter' would be a record that missed its mark and was the reason for Mausoleum to end their record deal. When singer Peter De Wint joined Ostrogoth in 1987, Crossfire called it quits.

Crossfire

Clockwise, from top right:
Eddy Verbruggen, Mantas (Venom),
Marc Van Caelenberghe (Crossfire),
Cronos (Venom).

Crossfire

*We used to rehearse frequently in my parents'
hall and then go out and play until we dropped.
We always rehearsed as if we were playing
live and gave it our all. Hell yeah,
we really rehearsed a lot.*

Peter De Wint, *Crossfire*

✝✝✝✝✝✝✝✝✝✝✝✝

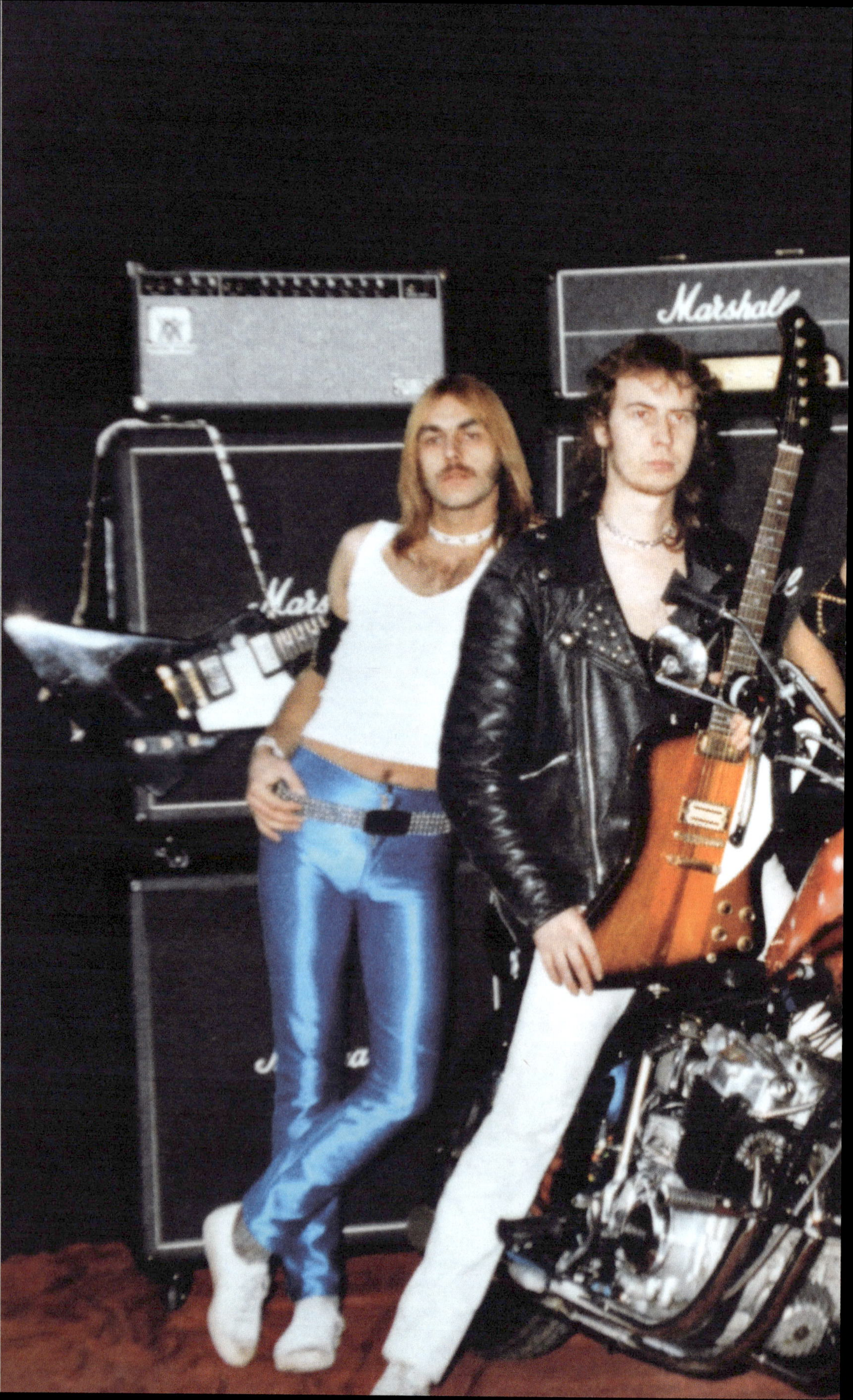
Marshall

MC THE AEGLES
Aartrijke

stelt voor
op 12 mei

HARDROCK TD
Warhead

met optreden van

CROSS-FIRE

in zaal Molenhof te Eernegem

AANVANG 20 U.
V.V.K. 120 F
KASSA 150 F.

| Cafe DE LIJMPOT | Coiffure MARLEEN | Cafe WESTENDE | SKOEBIDOE |

ZATERDAG 23 JUNI '84
TE ZOTTEGEM ZAAL ATC
(bij het station)

HEAVY METAL NIGHT
WITH
PHANTOM
ACID
CROSSFIRE

AANVANG : 19.00 u.   V.V.K. : 130,-
                                  INKOM : 180,-

Voorverkoopadressen :

THE SMASH : Zottegem.

ELYSEE : Kerksken.

BLACK OUT : Geraardsbergen.

MC THE DRIFTERS DENDERLEEUW

RICHTEN IN OP ZATERDAG 4 MEI 1985

1° HEAVY METAL AVOND MET :

CROSS FIRE

(MET BELGISCHE LP-PREMIERE "SECOND ATTACK")

WARHEAD

+ SUPPORT ACT

DIT ALLES GAAT DOOR IN ONZE FEESTTENT ACHTER ONS LOKAAL

CAFE PALLIETER STEENWEG OP AALST 2 , 9470 DENDERLEEUW

DEUREN 20.00 UUR
AANVANG 20.30 UUR
V.V.K. 100 BF

P.S. ER IS BEWAKING AANGEBRACHT

ZAT. 11 FEB. 84 ZAAL PERFA BURST
HEAVY METAL NIGHT WITH

CROSSFIRE

SUPPORT ACT: AXEL
+ METAL FUIF MET DJ UFO

V.V.K.: 149,5
INKOM: 149,5
BEGIN: 19 U

| HEAVY METAL CAFÉ TONNEKEN NIEUWERKERKEN | HARDROCK KROEG BLACK OUT GERAARDSB. | DISCOTHEEK ELYSEE KERKSKEN | DISCOTHEEK THE SMASH ZOTTEGEM |

Crossfire
en
Mercyful
Fate
satan tour

di. 28 sept.
20.00 uur
f 7,50

smalle haven 1

HOF TER LO BORGERHOUT ANTWERPEN ZONDAG 6 NOVEMBER '83 20.00 U.

VANDENBERG
OSTROGOTH
CROSSFIRE

tickets on sale at:
ANTWERPEN/BRABO RECORDS - GROTE MARKT 54 03/233.10.78

BRUSSEL: CAROLINE MUSIC - 20 PASSAGE ST HONORE - RUE DES FRIPERS 02/217.07.31
CAPTAIN MUSIC', 36 RUE DE L' ECUYER

AALST: SOLBEMOL - SLIJERSTR. 1 053/77.21.69
LEUVEN: CAMPUS - BONDGENOTENL. 30 016/23.92.00
HASSELT: HITJIP 'T.T. WIJK. C 19.011/22.69.57
ST.NIKLAAS/HERMANS PR ALBERTSTR.15 03/776.05.94

Scenergroep DICTUS Kjerkhout Tel.03/666.05.05

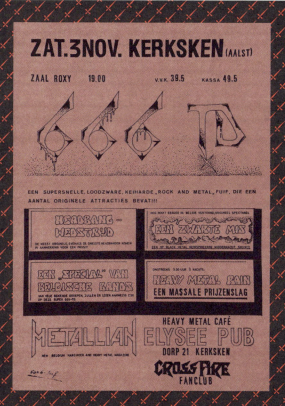

ZAT.3NOV. KERKSKEN (AALST)

ZAAL ROXY   19.00   V.V.K. 39.5   KASSA 49.5

EEN SUPERSNELLE, LOODZWARE, KEIHARDE ,ROCK AND METAL, FUIF, DIE EEN
AANTAL ORIGINELE ATTRACTIES BEVAT!!!

HEADBANG -
WEDSTRIJD
DE MEEST ORIGINELE, EVENALS DE SNELSTE HEADBANGER KOMEN
IN AANMERKING VOOR EEN PRIJS!!

EEN ZWARTE MIS
NOG NOOIT EERDER IN BELGIE VERTOOND, ORIGINEEL SPEKTAKEL
EEN OP BLACK METAL GEINSPIREERD MIDDERNACHT SHOWTJE

EEN "SPECIAL" VAN
BELGISCHE BANDS
VAN VELE BEKENDE GROEPEN, ZULLEN ER LEDEN AANWEZIG ZIJN
OP DEZE SUPER 666-TD.

HEAVY METAL KAIN
OMSTREEKS 3.00 UUR 'S NACHTS
EEN MASSALE PRIJZENSLAG

METALLIAN
NEW BELGIUM HARD-ROCK AND HEAVY METAL MAGAZINE

HEAVY METAL CAFÉ
ELYSEE PUB
DORP 21 KERKSKEN

CROSS FIRE
FANCLUB

FM ZØTTEGEM

PREZENTEERT OP

ZATERDAG 10 NOVEMBER 1984
A.T.C. ZOTTEGEM (nabij Station)

HEAVY METAL FESTIVAL

ROSENTHAL   AVALON

CROSSFIRE

FAITHFUL BREATH   in première met hun nieuwste LP "METAL BRAIN!"   TRANCE

Deuren : 16 uur   Voorverkoop : 350 fr.
Aanvang : 17 uur   Kassa : 400 fr.

THANKS TO   JOEPIE BETONROVER   MAUSOLEUM

Voorverkoop
THE SMASH - ZOTTEGEM   BILBO - BRUGGE
ELYSEE PUB - KERKSKEN   BLACK OUT - S'BERGEN
DE KEET - SERSKAMP   MISS - TIGRI - LESSINES
KIOSK - ZOTTEGEM   JEANS & PITTELEER - OUDENAARDE
SOLBEMOL - AALST   POPCENTER - KORTRIJK
MUSICMAN - GENT

VRIJDAG 26 OKT. '84

GEMEENTELIJKE FEESTZAAL
Bevrijdingsstraat, BALEN

Optreden van onze Belgische groepen

CROSS FIRE

BLACK WIDOW

LION SPRIDE

Aanvang : 19.30 uur

INKOM : 250,- F.   VOORVERKOOP : 220,- F.

Kaarten te verkrijgen in de BIERKELDER,
Stationsstraat 20, 2490 BALEN - Tel. 014-317159.

SHOCKWAVE
HEAVY METAL FESTIVAL
ZA. 22 OKT. LIMBURGHAL GENK 15.00 H DEUREN 14.00 H

RAVEN
KILLER

OSTROGOTH
BLACK WIDOW
CROSSFIRE · LION'S PRIDE

SPECIAL GUESTS

FEATURING PAUL MARIO DAY

TICKETS:
Voorverkoop   350 F
Dagverkoop   400 F

INFO:
EASY LIVIN 011 76.31.53
MAUSOLEUM RECORDS 03 235.21.12

IF IT AIN'T HEAVY
IT AIN'T ON
MAUSOLEUM

ZAT. 5 MEI 84 ZAAL HRITO AALST
Heavy Rock In Town FESTIVAL
Ingericht door Vriendenkring HRITO

BAD LIZZARD
AXEL
BLACK WIDOW
CROSSFIRE

TICKETS :

VVK :150,-   BEGIN :15 U
INKOM :180,-

EASY LIVIN V.Z.W. PRESENT

CROSS FIRE

HARD & HEAVY

WOENSDAG 11 NOVEMBER '81

ZAAL JAGERSBORG MAASMECHELEN
AANVANG 20.00 UUR

TICKETS 100 BF.
E.L. PASPOORT 70 BF.

INFO 011/763153
VRIJ VAN ZEGEL ART.198

VRIENDENKRING HRITO
RICHT IN:

VRIJ
PODIUM

OP: 23·4·'83   OM: 15u
MET: AXEL   REMARK
NEW VOICE   BLUE BIRD
    DINO'S GANG
IRON GRAY   RAZOR

MAIN ACT: OM 21u

CROSS-FIRE

KAARTEN: 80 Fr
INGANG: 100 Fr

Feestzaal HRITO
Welvaartstraat 70 · AALST

RAVEN
ACCEPT
Support CROSSFIRE

Vrijdag 24 SEPTEMBER 20u.
BRUGGE BEURSHALLE

VOORVERKOOP 300 · INGANG 350   RONSE : MUSIC BAR   TORHOUT : BUFFALO-GIPSY   MECHELEN : FOTOPLATENCENTER
BRUGGE : FLEMISH RECORD CENTER   LILLE : FNAC   ROESELARE : KLIJP   HASSELT : HITTIT
KORTRIJK : POPCENTER   BRUSSEL : METROPHONE   GENT : MUSIC MAN   LIER : CAROLINE MUSIC
OOSTENDE : BANKE O   ANTWERPEN : OPUS 1   LOKEREN : FONOTHEEK   OKAFLAGH : LIDO MUSIK
   LEUVEN : CAMPUS   AALST : SOLBEMOL   NAMUR : LA DROGUERIE

Flemish record store
Zuidzandstraat 27 BRUGGE

SOUND
New record shop
Niklaas Desparsstraat 3, 800 Brugge

Zeefdruk Steen 050 21 35 24

...GSKAART

OSTROGOTH
HEAVY METAL 84 Serskamp 4 AUG
ACID
KILLER
CROSS FIRE
Beauty and the Beast

4 AUGUSTUS 1984

Muziek vanaf 11 uur
Optredens vanaf 13,30 uur

Prijs : 400 BF voorverkoop   Plaats : De Witte Hoeve
450 BF kassa   Molenstraat · Serskamp

SECOND HEAVY METAL NIGHT

CROSS-FIRE
heavy metal

present

support act
TREASON

Zaterdag 12 november 1983   № 029
Zaal Rembrandt · Bottelaere

Aanvang 19.30 h   Inkom 140 fr.
    Voorverkoop 120 fr.
Verkoopadres: Tower Pub Dorp 32 Oosterzele

Killer: border-slashing assassins

Formed in late 1979, Killer quickly became the main force in a very young Belgian metal scene. Guitarist/vocalist Paul 'Shorty' Van Camp: "The New Wave Of British Heavy Metal was lurking around the corner and Belgium hadn't really caught on yet. Being the right band at the right time, we took a deep breath and jumped on the bandwagon. We soon got a record deal with the major WEA (Warner Elektra Atlantic). Especially in those early days, everything went smooth as silk. Back then, there wasn't much competition for us in Belgium, so we gathered a massive fan base. But since the metal scene was just starting out, we were pretty much doing everything ourselves: learning the ropes and exploring as we went along.

"With the release of our second album 'Wall Of Sound' in 1982, we started getting attention from abroad. That's when we signed to the legendary Mausoleum label. They were able to focus on Killer more than WEA, who just treated us like a shrimp in their big pond of bands."

"Killer and Ostrogoth both played at the first Heavy Sound festival in Bruges in 1983. In retrospect, the organisation was a bit amateurish, but that's how it was done back then. Apart from Torhout-Werchter there were no big festivals in Belgium. In fact, Heavy Sound were the first on the continent to organise a full-on metal festival. They just took the bet and did it."

"Even though we were based in the Antwerp region, we had our most loyal fanbase in West Flanders. It was logical. West Flanders has always been important, especially within the metal genre. Later Limburg joined in. Most of the students and self-proclaimed pseudo-intellectuals in the bigger Belgian cities rejected hard rock and heavy metal. We were constantly bashed by the press, and metal and hard rock were hardly ever played on radio and TV. Mainstream pop and rock festivals ignored us. It would be a couple of decades before the Werchter Festival finally booked a band like Metallica for the first time."

Still nix in eighty-six

The first serious dent in Killer's success came when Mausoleum went bankrupt. Just as the band's double live album was in the pipeline and pre-orders were pouring in. Plans for a major European tour were already in the works.

As Shorty recalls: "I truly think we were on the verge of a major international breakthrough. The interest from abroad seemed to be even greater than our popularity in Belgium. That makes sense, because we were playing so much that we were becoming an established act on the metal circuit. Across the border, fans were really eager to see Killer on stage. The Belgian audience has always been a bit more reserved and critical. But further south the people went crazy for us."

"'Still Alive in '85', our double live album, sadly never saw the light of day. We recorded a gig before a frenzied crowd in Antwerp with Dieter Dierks' (of Scorpions fame) mobile studio. We had even done the final mix and the artwork was ready to go to print. But because Mausoleum couldn't pay for the recordings, the tapes were locked away in the studio's vault." Not much later, the band had stickers made that said 'Still niks in '86'. We secretly hope that one day someone would blow up the vault and release the album. Officially - apart from a break in the 90s - Killer are still active. But they never really got over that setback.

I have a personal connection to the Maeke-Blyde. I saw Van Halen at that venue in the seventies. We went there by bus from Mechelen. Their legendary first album had just been released. A phenomenal performance, witnessed by just a handful of people. And then there was the fantastic show by Frank Marino and Mahogany Rush. Frank happens to be one of my all-time favourite guitarists. It was one of the best concerts I've ever seen. I was there as a guest with a journalist who wrote the Betonmolen column in Joepie magazine. *Paul 'Shorty' Van Camp, Killer*

A rainy Sunday afternoon in the Belgian provincial town of Heist-op-den-Berg. I'm looking for Harry's Studios. From the distance I can hear a banging noise. Something must be happening around here. An earthquake? Chinese nuclear tests perhaps? It turns out that, behind thick walls, Killer is finishing its new, third album called 'Shockwaves'. With his index fingers stuck in his ears, guitarist Shorty runs over to greet us. Out of breath, he drops his tired body down near the bar and grabs a bottle of mineral water from the vending machine. "We're not exactly Rush, we know that. But what we do is still a lot more complex than, say, Motörhead," he says.

Classical singers sometimes use a metronome to keep in tune. Killer record their albums according to the Richter scale, which is typically used to

† † † † † † † † † † † † †

Across the border, fans were really eager to
see us on stage. The Belgian audience has
always been a bit more reserved and critical.
But further south the people went crazy for us.

Paul 'Shorty' Van Camp, Killer

measure the strength of an earthquake. Shorty wasn't kidding. They are no Rush by any stretch of the imagination. But the new songs are Killer's most inventive yet. Twin guitar harmonies galore and drums that pound like a herd of wild horses galloping through the studio.

"A few weeks ago we did a dry run in another studio, but my guitar sounded too thin and lame," he says. "I'm not saying that Killer hangs out in the studio for months on end. We like to keep things fresh. Besides, the studio can be a dangerous place for us. Last night Spooky and I almost got into a fight. We ended up going to the pub to cool off and keep a safe distance from each other. That's why I'm sticking to mineral water today, see?"

Bassist and vocalist Spooky tells us how hard rock is in his heart and soul: "When the first bass player left, Shorty asked me to replace him. I still lived in Limburg at that time and travelled by train to band rehearsals almost every day. My wife didn't really like that. She was a bit worried that I would hang out in Mechelen with the Outlaws gang or other rough characters. You have to know that I have taken and thrown a few punches in the past. I didn't like her nagging all the time, so I divorced her. Does that prove how much I love being in this band? *Article from Joepie magazine*

ANDROMEDA'S HEADBANGERS DAVE STEWARD & HEAVY PIERRE & YVES VAN DE POPCENTER PRESENTEREN

OSTROGOTH
KILLER

ZAAL ZUUDHOVE KOEKELARE
ZATERDAG 31 MAART '84 – 20 uur

TICKETS:
– POPCENTER (OOSTENDE/KORTRIJK)
– SCOOBY DOO (KOEKELARE)
– NONSTOP MUSIC CENTER (KOEKELARE)
– DING DONG (KORTEMARK)
– THE BARREL PUB (GISTEL)

– BILBO (BRUGGE)
– BUFFALO (TORHOUT)
– DE SEULE (ZERKEGEM)
– OOSTENDE PLATEN CENTRUM (OOSTENDE)

POPCENTER, CHRISTINASTRAAT 147, 8400 OOSTENDE

V.U. HEADBANGERS, POSTBUS 175, OOSTENDE – VRIJ VAN ZEGEL ART. 198.7

MAEKEBLYDE POPERINGE
Zaterdag 5 December '81, 20u.

New Abasti Concerts presenteert

KILLER
THE RAVES
BUZZARD

KAARTEN
GEERVIK – De Markiezin
IMOELMUNSTER – De Coutershoe
WERNK – De Stogge – Kribbe?
TURNHOUT – Melody Maker
IZEGEM – De Mexico
OBERLIJN – 't Haantje
TIENEN – Happy Days
MIDDELKERKE – The Llans
KOEKELARE – Plet Geln – Klop
KORTEMARK – Sine Sond

KOEKSLAVA – Koekelare Shoes
SMOLGA – Bilbo
TIELT – De Marbo
ROUPAIDE – Popcenter
SERKEGHEM – Kacey – Norpoebel
DIKSMUIDE – 't Kabaretstik
VLAMERTINGA – Barrow
WANIGARE – Moscow
OOSTENDE – C-Sle

de platenzaak voor popliefhebbers

VRIJ VAN ZEGEL CULT.DOEL.

Zeefdruk Steen 050.21 35 24

ZATERDAG 19 MAART 1983
Zaal CONCORDIA, Stationstraat 75 Eernegem

IN CONCERT
STAINLESS STEEL
KILLER

m.m.v. Radio Activity

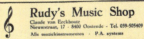

Rudy's Music Shop
Claude van Eeckhoute
Nieuwstraat, 17 - 8400 Oostende - Tel. 059-505409
Alle muziekinstrumenten - P.A. systems

Café Central   bij Jean-Marie
                       Dorpstraat 84 - ETTELGEM

Voor een frisse pint · Muziek voor jong en oud.

VOORVERKOOP ADRESSEN :
Café CENTRAL Ettelgem
Café CONCORDIA, Eernegem
"B. Q. Brabantstraat 3, Oostende

Café WELKOM, Stationstr. 34, Lissewege
Café CADZAND, Cadzandstraat, Oostende
Jeugdcafé SKOEBIDOE, Koekelare
RUDY'S MUSICSHOP, Oostende

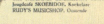

Ostrogoth and the Eagles

Along with Killer, Ostrogoth can be considered the godfathers of Belgian metal. Formed in 1980, they were one of the first bands to jump on the British heavy metal bandwagon. Drummer Mario 'Grizzly' Pauwels: "In the beginning we were still trying to find our own style. The least you can say is that our music wasn't radio friendly. We did everything ourselves, including promotion: word of mouth, flyers, posters, you name it. We scanned the scene for opportunities to play our first gigs or organised them ourselves. It was quite adventurous and we rehearsed like madmen. We often played at the Zuidhove in Koekelare, which regularly hosted mini-festivals with the cream of Belgian metal. This venue soon became known throughout Flanders and attracted large crowds. The organisers were members of the Eagles biker gang from Aartrijke, who were experienced in organising gigs. Ostrogoth became a kind of house band there."

In 1983, Ostrogoth were the first Belgian metal band to perform live at the inaugural edition of the Heavy Sound festival in Bruges. In spite of its small size and convivial atmosphere, the festival attracted a large number of visitors from abroad. Grizzly: "We had to hit the stage at 11 in the morning for a 25-minute set, but we received a warm welcome and a great response from the crowd. It was definitely the start of bigger projects for us! On the same day we also released our long-awaited 'Full Moon's Eyes' EP. Our label had arranged for a hundred copies to be available after our show."

Behind the scenes, Ostrogoth had been rehearsing hard for three years, and it was paying off. On their first mini-album, the Ghent collective presented powerful heavy metal with a strong sense of melody. If you liked amazing guitar work with distinctive twin solos, inventive breaks and a vocalist who commands respect, you simply had to love Ostrogoth.

One pub, one crowd

Drummer Grizzly recalls, "Steppenwolf and Blue Cheer were the first bands that really inspired me to make my own music. I found punk interesting because it gave the rock scene a kick in the butt at the time. But musically it didn't really appeal to me. As a musician I think it is important to be as good as you can be technically to enjoy your work."

Ostrogoth

Ostrogoth is sometimes compared to Scorpions or Judas Priest. I have no problem with that. After all, those are two of my favourite bands.

Mario 'Grizzly' Pauwels

© Rudi De Danckt

© Rudy De Doncker

"The atmosphere at many pub shows was very different from today. There was no division into different genres and venues. You had one pub and everyone went there to have a beer. At gigs, for example, I notice that people who don't like heavy metal openly show their disapproval. Because there was no club scene in Belgium, you'd often play festivals where other types of bands were playing. This sometimes led to crazy situations. Anyway, it wasn't always peace and love, I can tell you that."

"There was a lot of competition between bands too. As soon as an international act came to Belgium, there was a tug-of-war to be the support act. Of course there was jealousy between the bands, after all it took more than just good music to get noticed internationally." *Based on an interview in Joepie magazine*

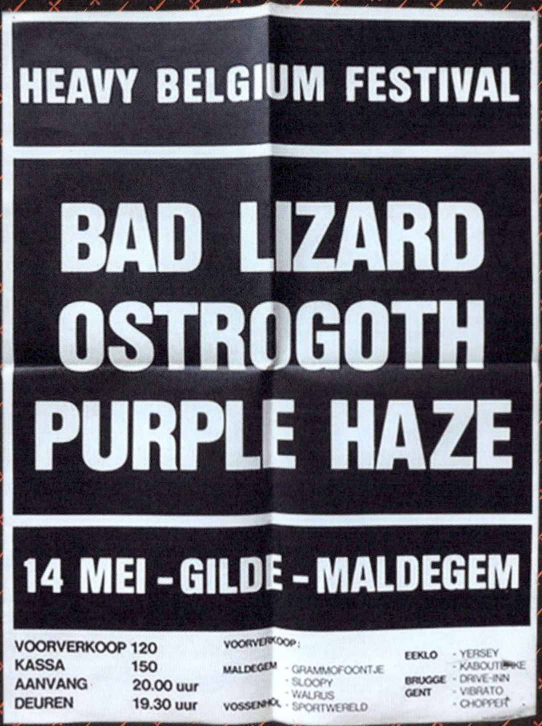

HEAVY BELGIUM FESTIVAL

BAD LIZARD
OSTROGOTH
PURPLE HAZE

14 MEI - GILDE - MALDEGEM

VOORVERKOOP 120	VOORVERKOOP :	EEKLO	- YERSEY
KASSA 150			- KABOUTERKE
AANVANG 20.00 uur	MALDEGEM - GRAMMOFOONTJE	BRUGGE	- DRIVE-INN
DEUREN 19.30 uur	- SLOOPY	GENT	- VIBRATO
	- WALRUS		- CHOPPER
	VOSSENHOL - SPORTWERELD		

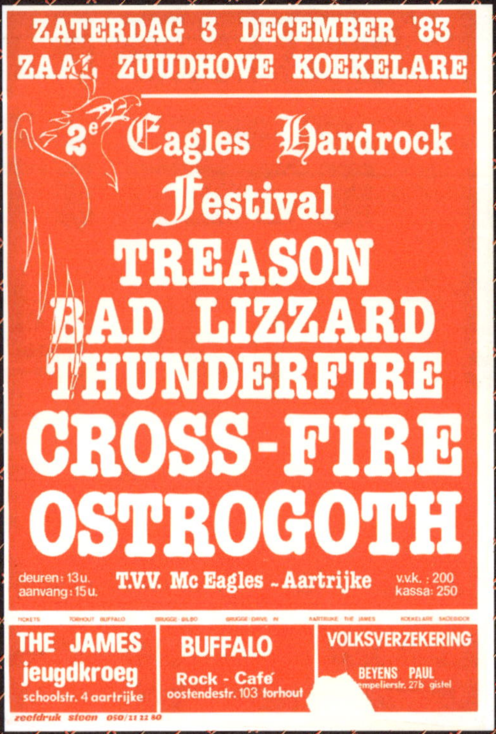

ZATERDAG 3 DECEMBER '83
ZAAL ZUUDHOVE KOEKELARE

2e Eagles Hardrock Festival
TREASON
BAD LIZZARD
THUNDERFIRE
CROSS-FIRE
OSTROGOTH

deuren: 13u.
aanvang: 15u.
T.V.V. Mc Eagles - Aartrijke
v.vk. : 200
kassa: 250

THE JAMES jeugdkroeg
schoolstr. 4 aartrijke

BUFFALO
Rock - Café
oostendestr. 103 torhout

VOLKSVERZEKERING
BEYENS PAUL
impelierstr. 27b gistel

zeefdruk steen 050/11 11 40

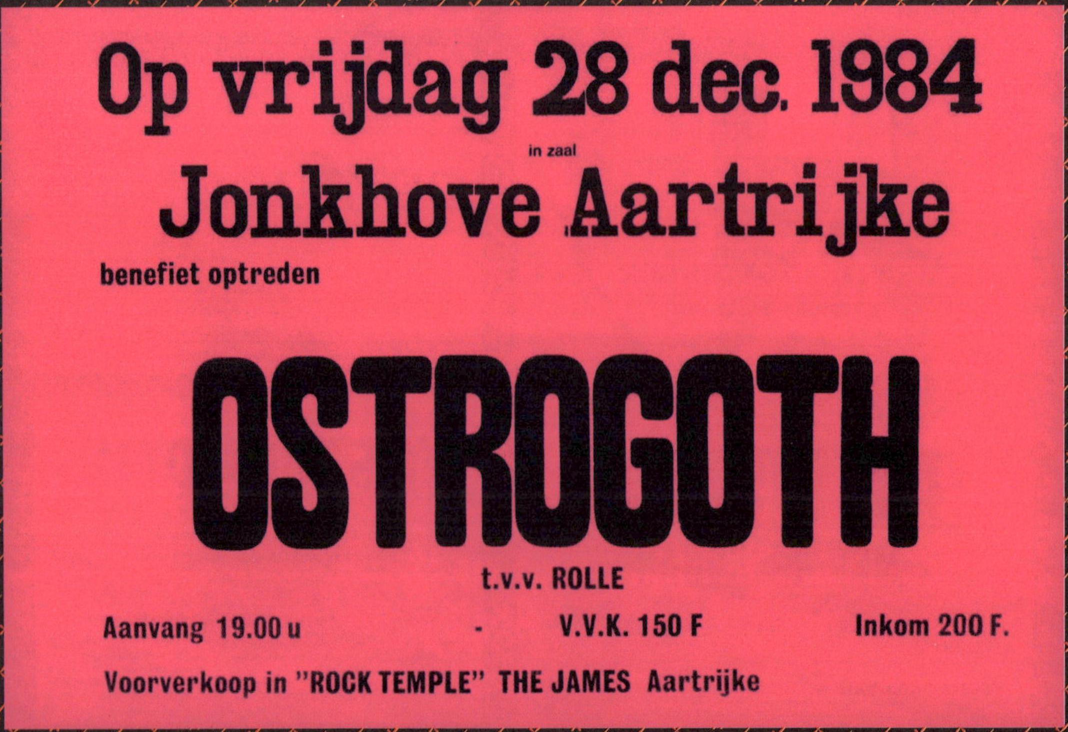

Op vrijdag 28 dec. 1984

in zaal

Jonkhove Aartrijke

benefiet optreden

OSTROGOTH

t.v.v. ROLLE

Aanvang 19.00 u - V.V.K. 150 F Inkom 200 F.

Voorverkoop in "ROCK TEMPLE" THE JAMES Aartrijke

METAL BATTLE

1 DEC.'84

TWEE MAANDE-LIJKS

VORTEX

AXEL
OMEN
TOP 5

MERCYFUL FATE POSTER

bad lizard

40 FR.

②

crossfire METALLICA motörhead

Heavy Metal magazine

TyTaN

Metal News 4 - Maart/April '85
België:80Bf/Nederland:4f50

32 blz Staal!

Afscheidsconcert satan

crossfire
powerage
metallica
buzzard
lions pride

The magazine for real Headbangers

OP VRIJDAG 28 DEC. TE Aartrijke

BENEFIET OPTREDEN

OSTROGOTH

T.V.V. "ROLLE"

IN ZAAL JONKHOVE

AANVANG : 19 UUR.   V.V.K : 150
                    INKOM : 200

HEAVY BELGIUM FESTIVAL

BAD LIZARD
OSTROGOTH
PURPLE HAZE

Zaterdag 14 mei 1983 - Gilde - Maldegem

Voorverkoop 120 fr.   Aanvang 20.00 u.
Kassa 150 fr.   Deuren 19.30 u.

KEIHARDE ROCKFUIF

IN ZAAL ZUUDHOVE, KOEKELARE

ZATERDAG 4 DECEMBER 1982
aanvang 20 uur

PURPLE HAZE
OSTROGOTH
MET DISCOBAR

T.V.V. M.C. THE EAGLES

Voorverkoop 120 fr.   Avond zelf 150 fr.

HIER VOORVERKOOP

AARTRIJKE   ZATERDAG 21 APRIL 1984
Café THE JAMES   Exclusief enig optreden van

OSTROGOTH

Only for owr fans and friends
This concert is dedicated
to MC The Aegles

INKOM : 80 Fr.   Aanvang 21 uur
                      Slechts 150 kaarten verkrijgbaar

druk raf vlamynck-plaisier - eernegem

OSTROGOTH

EP **Full Moon's Eyes** Bone 128310
LP **Ecstasy and Danger** Skull 8319 + TAPE
LP **Too Hot** Skull 8374 + TAPE

Management   Fanclub   Ostrogoth Merchandise
                  Geuens Hendrik
                  Lommelsesteenweg 25 bus 1
                  3970 Leopoldsburg (B)
Van Huyghem Herman Samoy Frederic   Bogaert Arthur
Strijandstraat 36   7, Petite Avenue Léopold Jules van Biesbroeckstraat 173
1686 Gooik (Belgium) 1330 Rixensart (B)   9219 Gent (Belgium)
054/56 77 19

Kortrijk reclaims its fame among hard rockers

In 1983, Kortrijk's rocking hard again, and it's not just the locals getting in on the action. Young people are coming in from Roeselare and Poperinge to let their hair down at the hard rock pubs in Kortrijk. According to Geert Cuvelier, who runs the Mady, one of Kortrijk's four hard rock pubs, the concentration of these pubs in the Spoorweglaan, with an offshoot near the railway station, is responsible for the current success.

Headbangers have had to wait a long time for a genuine hard rock pub in Kortrijk. Admittedly, the genre had its beginnings in various youth clubs, culminating in The Chopper for the hard core. The pub was an overwhelming success, so emulation was not out of the question. However, the success was temporarily interrupted and the last hard rock pub closed its doors in the mid-1980s. Poperinge, the other epicentre, also experienced a serious decline.

But it didn't take long for the scene to rejuvenate. Within two years, four new hard rock pubs opened in Kortrijk. Three of them cater to traditional rock fans. For those who want to listen to the crossover between hard rock and punk, such as speedcore and thrash metal, there is De Tunnel. This new rabid variant of the genre appealed especially to younger fans.

The reputation of the Kortrijk nightlife in hard rock circles is nothing new. After all, the genre rooted here in the early 1970s. When the Popcenter record store (now known as Musicman) opened in 1972, it helped to boost the popularity of the heavier genre in the region. From the start, the store offered an exquisite selection of hard rock records from around the world. The place became a haven for hard rock fans in the immediate vicinity of Kortrijk and beyond.

Hard rock pubs are on the rise again in Kortrijk. All but one are located on the same street, not far from the railway station. Cuvelier: "The concentration of pubs is crucial to attract people from outside the region. Otherwise they wouldn't come here. And I have to admit that the chart success of bands like Bon Jovi and Europe also helped to

increase the popularity of hard rock in general. The downside of those hit records is that people expect you to play them ... ad nauseam".

As for today's hard rock crowd? "They're chillin' out more," Cuvelier notes. Less aggression is cool, but he does miss the wild vibe of the old days. The hard rock pubs in Kortrijk are on the rise again, with the Mady attracting a hard rock audience of all ages.
(Article from newspaper Het Nieuwsblad, late 80s)

Pubs in the Tolstraat, Kortrijk (1983)

In the summer of 1985, I sometimes took the train to the seaside. I had never really travelled before. That same year, the Stenen Tijdperk pub in Kortrijk closed its doors. Stiene, who ran the pub, opened a hard rock club called De President in Blankenberge. During the summer, the coastal hotspot was overrun with tourists, biker gangs and hard rockers from all over the world. Kris Maes, singer of the band Dreft, and I decided to spend the night there.

After a few beers, I must have fallen asleep on one of the benches in De President. When I woke up, I found myself under a pile of coats, with Stiene grinning from behind the bar. Apparently a member of the Hells Angels had fired a shot with a riot gun in the middle of the night. Everyone in and around the bar was arrested. I was lucky enough to be overlooked by the cops. The real culprit had disappeared, so my mate Kris was released in the morning. Apparently this sort of thing happened almost every day during the 'high season'. *Hans Verbeke*

Za. 21 Mei 1983 Brugge 11h.-21h.

HEAVY SOUND FESTIVAL 83

Brugge-SV/L Voetbalstadion (800 m. van station)

OSTROGOTH
KILLER
VIVA
GOLDEN EARRING
WARNING
URIAH HEEP
BARON ROJO
GARY MOORE (IAN PAICE)
SURPRISE

VOORVERKOOP
AALST Solbemal
AALTER Music House
ANTWERPEN Opus
ARLON Toys Club
BRUGGE Music Man
BRUSSEL Metrophone
CHARLEROI Lido Music
DE PANNE Serenade

EEKLOO Mattys
GENK Cinderella
GENT Music Man
HASSELT Hittip
HERENTALS Disc-Music
IEPER Happy Days
KORTRIJK Popcentr
LEUVEN Campus
LIEGE Caroline Music

LOKEREN Fonotheek
MENEN De Krimson
MECHELEN Center Fonoplaten
MONS Music Square
NAMUR La Disquerie
OOSTENDE Rainbow
POPERINGE Hoppebel
ROESELARE Klup
RONSE Music Bar

ST TRUIDEN Music Center
TIELT De Maribel
TORHOUT Buffalo
TOURNAI Tournai Disques
TURNHOUT Center

PREVENTE ETRANGER
AACHEN Kim Records (D)
KOLN HPS-Promotion (D)
LILLE Fnac (F)
PARIS Fnac Forum (F)
LUXEMBOURG Plakka Buttek -L-

EINDHOVEN : Van Leest (N)
MAASTRICHT : Kantoren De Limburger (N)
ROTTERDAM : Rotterdams Nieuwsblad (N)
SLUIS Paul's Music Center (N)
AMSTERDAM : De Nieuwe Muziekh

Zeefdruk Steen 050 21 35 24

✝✝✝

Heavy Sound Festival 1983

The Heavy Sound festival sees the light of day in 1983 when a thundering train loaded with heavy metal drops its cargo on the former football ground of Cercle Brugge. With a lot of perseverance, but no script whatsoever, volunteers toil day and night to fulfil a titanic task: to build Europe's first metal festival on the green—from out of nowhere.

Residents, bars and restaurants in the neighbourhood and local authoroties are both anxious and curious. What would become of their peaceful town when 5,000 metalheads descended upon it?

For the press, this is is a godsend: photographers and journos try to capture every minute of the spectacle in rich detail. And oh, the hunger of the crowd! Like ravenous beasts, they devour every riff, every beat of hard rock hurled their way, craving more with each passing moment. In the crucible of sound and energy, a new tradition was forged—a festival born from the passion and sweat of its creators.

It all started when 21-year-old Joris De Clerck opened his first pub in Bruges. It wasn't long before the place became a magnet for local talent, among them a band whose thunderous metal shook the rafters and captured hearts. This band was Acid, and their arrival heralded the beginning of a new era. Joris helped the Bruges group to produce their debut 7", 'Hooked On Metal'. When he joined them in organising gigs at the Bruges Trade Hall, the Heavy Sound crew was born.

The ball began to roll, and momentum built with each successful show, which would culminate in a grand plan and ultimately, the first Heavy Sound festival. Joris threw himself into the fray, unaware of the magnitude of what he was about to unleash. The chosen location? The run-down football ground of Cercle Brugge. Despite naysayers predicting that the stalls would never withstand the impact, the organisers remained steadfast in their determination to bring their masterplan to life.

Boldly defying all conventions, the first open-air metal festival in continental Europe becomes a roaring success. What it lacked in professional polish, it made up for in sheer passion and determination. As the gates swung open, a flood of 5,000 metal-hungry fans surged in. The large contingent of French and British metalheads present proved the growing need for a truly heavy festival across the continent. But the festival's triumph wasn't just a stroke of luck. Behind the scenes, a dedicated squad of volunteers waged a relentless campaign to spread the word far and wide. Throughout France, Germany and the Netherlands, posters adorned every available surface, while ads found their way into the pages of countless magazines and fanzines.

At the helm of this crusade was none other than Joris, a young guy who embarked on a solo tour of England, personally knocking on the doors of major record labels to secure the cream of the metal scene. Back in Bruges, the fax machines worked overtime as contracts were signed and deals were sealed. Meanwhile, partners Luc Waeyaert and Rik Stael, veterans of the music scene with New Abasti, lent their expertise to the cause. Though their roles were initially modest, confined to poster duty and fieldwork, their potential was unmistakable. And shine they would, for as the festival grew from

> ✠✠✠✠✠✠✠✠✠✠✠✠✠
>
> The run-down football ground of Cercle Brugge. Despite naysayers predicting that the stalls would never withstand the impact, the organisers remained steadfast in their determination to bring their masterplan to life. Boldly defying all conventions, the first open-air metal festival in continental Europe becomes a roaring success.
>
> ✠✠✠✠✠✠✠✠✠✠✠✠✠

strength to strength, Luc and Rik would emerge as key players.

As the festival kicked off, it was immediately plagued by a slew of sound problems. The assembled press scribbled furiously in their notebooks, detailing the faltering speakers, the uneven sound mix and, in a truly bizarre twist, the faint strains of disco music that danced through the air during French band Warning's set. It seemed that someone had left the background music channel open on one of the sound towers, casting a shadow over several sets, including those of Belgian heroes Ostrogoth and Killer. Even the German band Viva, stepping in for the scheduled headliners Accept, found themselves struggling with the unstable sound system. But amidst the chaos, Viva's frontwoman Barbara Schenker captured the hearts of many fans, as the sole woman to grace the stage on that tumultuous day.

The night of the festival drew near, and rumours swirled about a surprise act, with whispers of Lemmy himself roaming the festival grounds. The possibility of a Motörhead performance electrified the crowd. But it soon became clear that Mr Kilmister hadn't come for an impromptu show. As Lemmy had journeyed across the channel just to catch the vibe of their new festival, the organisers seized this golden opportunity with both hands. So, when the time came for the big reveal, it was not Motörhead who took the stage, but the Canadians of Anvil, taking the crowd by storm as the surprise act. And who better to join in the festivities than the legendary Lemmy himself? As the crowd erupted, he ascended into the evening sky in a hot air balloon. With a mischievous twinkle in his eye, he showered the ecstatic audience below with towels bearing the festival logo. Guerrilla marketing avant la lettre, and a magical moment that would be etched into the annals of Belgian music history.

According to the fanzines from the era, Anvil were the band that elevated the festival to its legendary status. While other headliners like Uriah Heep, Gary Moore, and Golden Earring leaned towards hard rock, Anvil brought unpolished, brutal metal energy. Their performance, backed by a well-tuned sound system, had the crowd's neck muscles sore from relentless headbanging.

Yet, the finale didn't go as planned. Gary Moore, slated to close the show, encountered backstage tensions earlier in the day and demanded that his 'personal space' be respected. Anvil playfully put the man in his place, causing a bit of a stir. When delays pushed Moore's set hours later, he refused to perform. As a result, he swapped places with the friendly Madrilenians of Baron Rojo.

After Gary Moore's set, the festival ground began to thin out. But those who stayed were treated to one final highlight of the evening. Baron Rojo set the stage alight with their classic Spanish-spoken hard rock, reigniting the spirits of the rain-soaked fans one last time. *Larga vida al rock and roll!* As the night drew to a close, you could feel that this festival edition left everyone craving for more.

The air buzzed with potential, promising fewer sound problems and even bigger metal names in future editions. While this inaugural edition leaned more towards hard rock with its lineup of classic and renowned acts, it still faces competition for the title of 'first European metal festival' from Kortrijk's Wheelpop. However, that debate would be put to rest in the following year's edition.

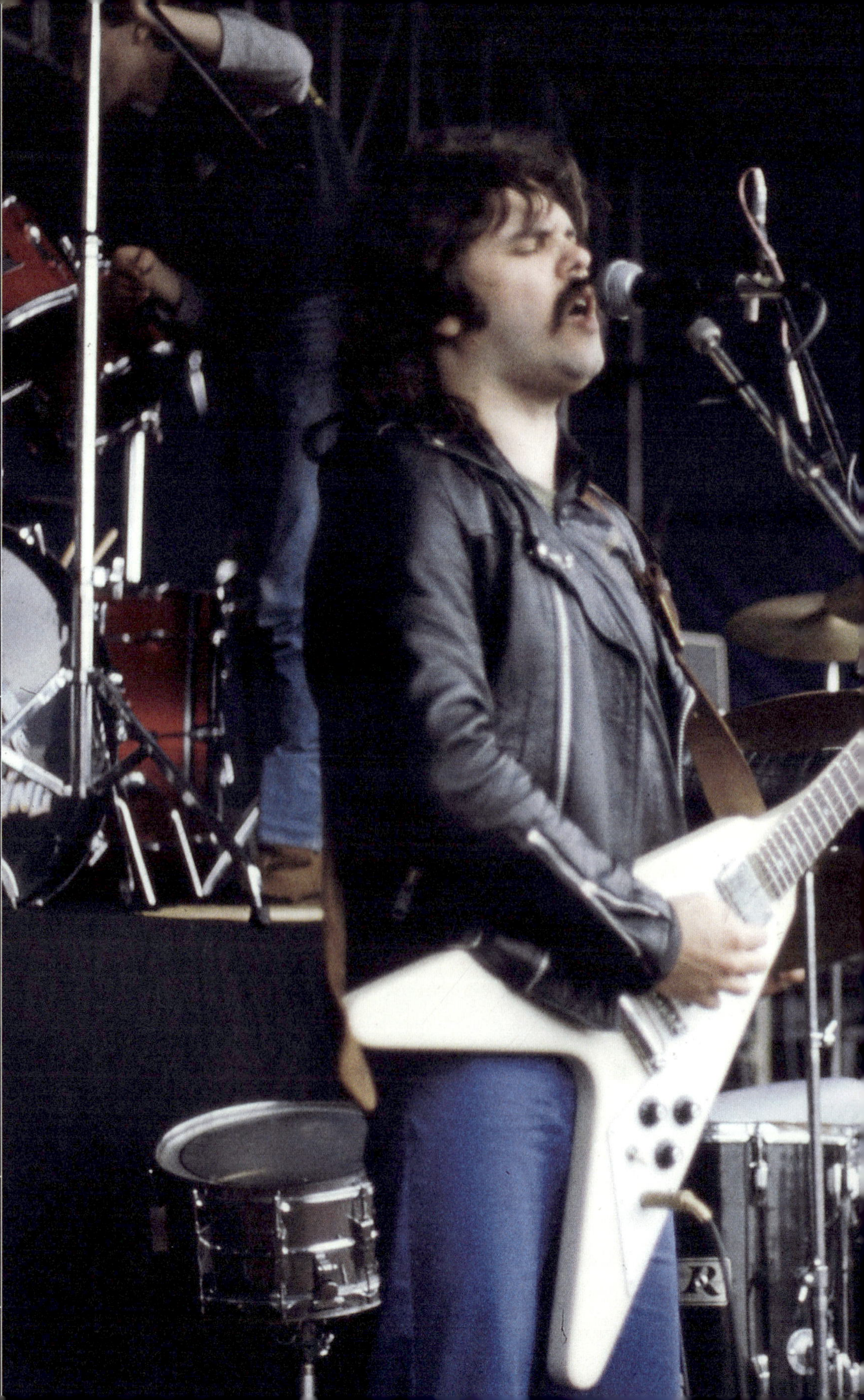

Picture this: I'd just turned fifteen, heading to a heavy metal festival in Bruges, Belgium. It's 1983—the era of bulky cassette recorders. Mine? Cunningly conceiled in my bag, wrapped in aluminum foil and stashed among my festival gear. Bringing recording equipment to a festival was a strict no-go.

There, amidst the crowd, lurks the icon himself, Lemmy, puffing away on one of the largest reefers I'd ever seen. The sound of Viva fills the air, with Barbara Schenker captivating the audience's hearts. After the show, I strike up a conversation with her, and to my amazement, she

hands us two backstage passes. Mine reads 'Friends of Viva'! Oh, those were the days...

But the surprises don't end there. Backstage, I catch glimpses of Lips and Anvil's crew. Could they be the surprise act? When they finally take the stage, we go apeshit! Despite the less-than-perfect sound, Canadian powerhouse Anvil put on a performance for the history books. And you know what? Sound quality is overrated. My crackling cassette recordings from that day are the living proof. *Phil.P*

Heavy Sound Festival '83 - Brugge

Viva

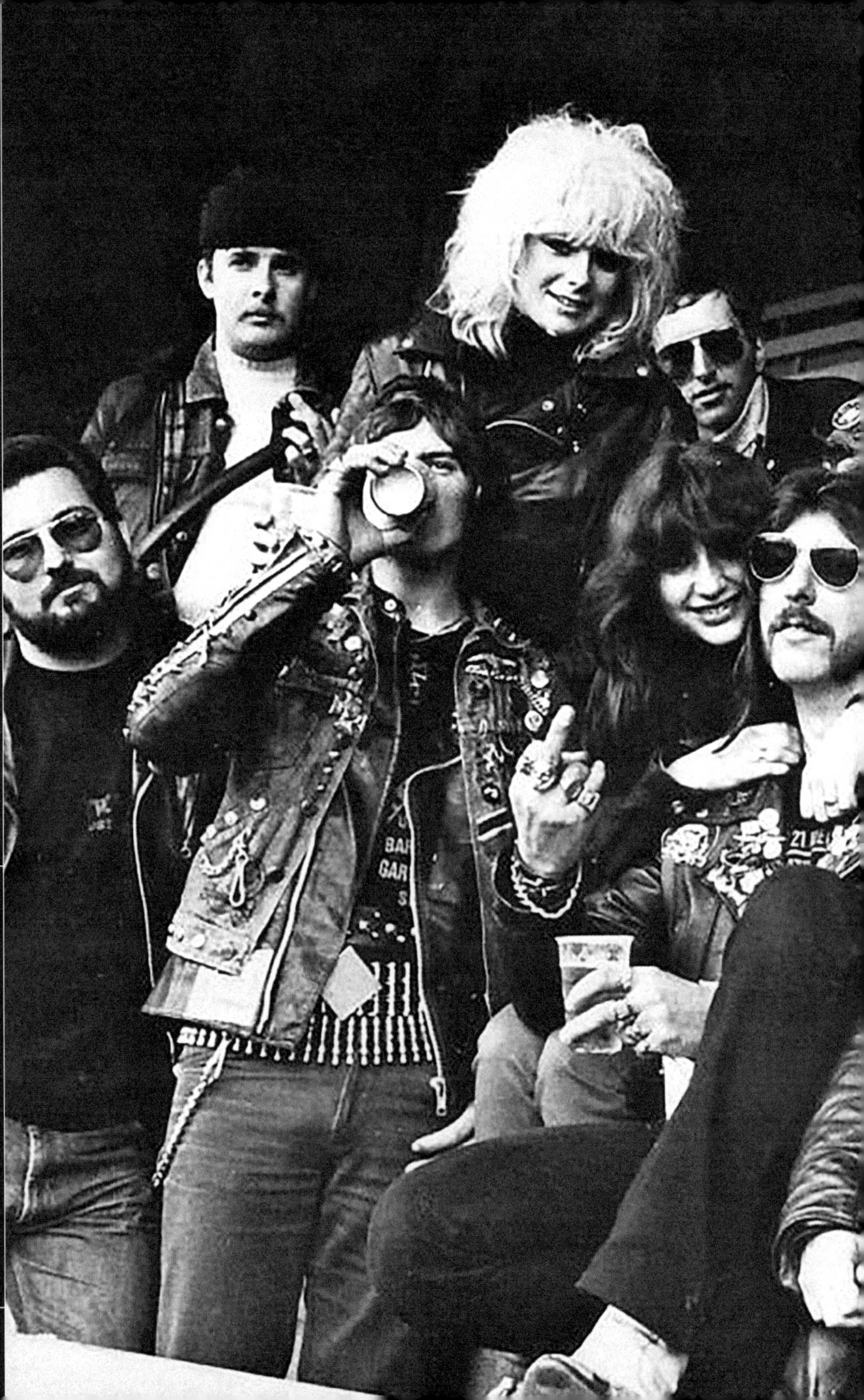

Heavy Sound Festival '83 - Crew 21-05-1983

© Joseph Carlucci

𝕽𝖆𝖉𝖆𝖗 𝕷𝖔𝖛𝖊 𝖔𝖗 ... 𝕳𝖆𝖙𝖊?

Opinions on Golden Earring's show at Heavy Sound Festival 1983 were mixed. With a decade-old hit like 'Radar Love', the band's longevity was un-deniable. However, despite pristine sound quality, their performance failed to ignite much energy among the crowd. It seemed the audience's thirst for heavier tunes played against the Earrings' favour.

Warning

Through the Lens of a Metal Maestro

My journey into concert photography began with iconic acts like The Police and Queen, capturing their essence at Forest National in Brussels between 1979 and 1980. However, it was my first peek behind the scenes at an Iron Maiden show in Brussels in 1982 that truly sparked my passion. Steve Harris himself handed me an All Areas Access pass for the Reading Festival in August 1982, and from that moment on, there was no turning back.

As the 90s dawned, I found myself stepping back from the photography scene, only snapping shots at the request of bands I befriended. Concert conditions grew increasingly challenging, with a flood of photographers vying for the perfect shot, and strict limitations on shooting time. In the eighties, the situation was different. There were fewer photographers, mainly because equipment was pricey, and developing films was a cumbersome task. Money was tight back then. I couldn't afford to stock up on films. So, you know, sometimes I'd burn through them too fast and end up kicking myself. For me, photography was always driven by passion rather than profit.

Man, the first Heavy Sound Festival? It was an absolute blast. Back in '83, if you wanted to catch some hard rock or metal, you had to haul yourself off to Donington or Reading in the UK, or Dortmund in Germany. But then Bruges came as a revelation. And in February '84, I stumbled upon the Maeke-Blyde, where Venom and Metallica hit the stage for the very first time in Belgium.

I'd been a Metallica fan since their first demo tape dropped in 1982. Back then, hardly anyone knew who they were. You had to scour those special record shops, and dig the expensive import crates for their album. I became a regular at the Maecke-Blyde, thanks to Luc and the Abasti crew pushing metal bands. I'd lived in Brussels for most of my life, but West Flanders was where the action was at. And Poperinge? Bands from all over tearing it up on stage: pure magic.

After hanging with Helloween back in '86, I created these comic pumpkin characters for them. They were used on their albums, for their merchandising, and then I also designed some album covers for the band.
Frederick Moulaert

†††††††††††††

Lemmy arrived at the festival in
a white limo. And as a surprise
act, he took off in a hot air balloon
and hovered over the festival.
He threw towels with the Heavy
Sound Flying V festival logo
down on the crowd. Fantastic!

Marnix Bruyneel

†††††††††††††

Lemmy

© Frederick Morlaert

© Joseph Cartucci

Baron Rojo

© Frederick Moulaert

© Frederick Moulaert

+++++++++++++

Baron Rojo closed the festival
with a party. A rock-solid
finale, even if a lot of people had
already left because of the bad
weather, or had to catch their
last train home.

Pat Genk

+++++++++++++

White-hot with rage: the Gary Moore incident

In the early 1980s, Rik Stael and I were the dynamic duo behind Abasti
Concerts, daring to bring hard rock to the forefront when others shied away.
Conversations with Joris De Clerck birthed the idea of a hard rock festival.
When we stumbled upon posters for the first Heavy Sound festival, Joris
enlisted our help backstage. The debut edition was a bit of a rough ride on the
organisational front. Picture this: a spotlight crashes down just inches from

Gary Moore. That's what we got for using cheap rigging material. Needless to say, Gary was less than thrilled, and his wrath had consequences. His agency blacklisted us, and we could no longer book bands on their roster. The next year, Joris, Rik and I joined forces once more, doubling down on our commitment. I even quit my day job to focus 100% on making the festival a success.
Luc Waeyaert

Heavy Sound Festival '83 - Brugge

Anvil

© Frederick Moulaert

Surprise Surprise

In the spring of '83, as a writer for Sanctuary magazine, I travelled to Bruges. It was Friday, the 20th of May, and the city held the promise of an adventure unlike any other. Our accommodation? None other than the home of Eddy Verbruggen, a prominent figure in the metal scene of the era. We made our way to the Gistelsesteenweg, where Eddy lived with his wife at the time. Stepping through the doorway, we were greeted by the sight of a true music aficionado's haven. The walls were adorned with posters of rock gods, and the air was thick with the scent of vinyl. Eddy's record collection struck us with awe. The man entertained us with tales that would make even the most seasoned rocker's head spin. As the evening unfolded, we made our way to the stadium. Upon arrival, the surprise act advertised for the next day was revealed to us as none other than Anvil. Our hearts pounding with anticipation, we returned to Eddy's headquarters, where we feasted our ears on the latest metal albums until daylight came.

It was drizzling at the festival, but we had our booth in the covered area and got backstage access. Ostrogoth presented their 'Full Moon's Eyes' EP on the square, which I bought immediately. Schlepping the record around all day was well worth it. As the festivities kicked off, rumours circulated about Killer's uncertain slot due to time constraints. Nevertheless, they managed to squeeze in a short set. Warning from France had sound issues, with ghostly echoes of Deep Purple's 'Highway Star' still playing over the PA during their first song. Viva fronted by Barbara Schenker were excellent, but we skipped Golden Earring. Not heavy enough. Uriah Heep, with the ever-friendly Mick Box, delivered a great performance, setting the stage for the surprise act's thunderous entrance. Anvil's showmanship was unparalleled, with Lips shredding a vibrator across the strings of his flying V. Gary Moore swapped places with Baron Rojo on the bill due to a tight schedule. Moore, already on edge, faced further frustration when a spotlight took an unexpected tumble, missing him by a couple of inches.

After their set, Moore and his band vanished into the night, heading off to Pinkpop the following afternoon. Meanwhile, Baron Rojo took the stage, igniting the festival grounds with a fiery finale. Lemmy of Motörhead made a surprise appearance, drawn by his friendship with Eddy Verbruggen.

As the night wore on, we anticipated a restful night at Eddy's place. However, an argument between Eddy and his wife dashed our hopes. We'd only just found refuge in one of the band trailers, when we were woken up by a banging on the door. The stage needed dismantling, and every able body was called to action—including us. With our tasks complete, we trudged towards Bruges train station, eager to catch the first train to Genk. Exhausted but satisfied, we carried memories with us that would last a lifetime... *Pat Genk*

© Rudy De Doncker

✝✝✝✝✝✝✝✝✝✝✝✝✝

The Heavy Sound Festival was the turning point.
From then on I realised that the audience really
came for us. No matter how long we played, they
stayed glued to our lips. Lemmy gave me a sneak
preview of the new Motörhead album 'Another
Perfect Day' on his Walkman. Whatta day!

Steve 'Lips' Kudlow, Anvil

✝✝✝✝✝✝✝✝✝✝✝✝✝

*Pete Decock (pictured right),
aka T-Bone from Acid: a
massive Anvil fan waiting for
the band coming off stage.*

FEBRUARI '83 jaargang 1

Slechts 30 Bfr

KROH

NIEUW ALTERNATIEF ROESTVRIJ BETONBLAD!!

S.ANCTUARY

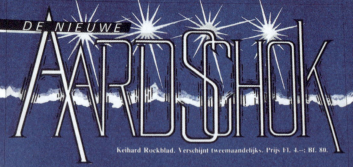

DE NIEUWE

AARDSCHOK

Keihard Rockblad. Verschijnt tweemaandelijks. Prijs Fl. 4,--; Bf. 80.

GARY MOORE
FRANKRIJK DEEL II
ANVIL
ROCK GODDESS
HEAVY SOUND Fest.
IRON MAIDEN
SAMSON
VANDENBERG
ACEIUM
JAPAN DEEL III
MINI POSTER
AARDSCHOKDAG
DIAMOND HEAD
PRETTY MAIDS

AUG. 1983 6

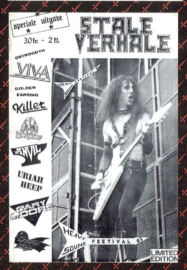

speciale uitgave
30 fr. - 2 fl.

STALE VERHALE

OSTROGOTH
VIVA
GOLDEN EARRING
Killer
WARNING
ENVIL
URIAH HEEP
GARY MOORE

HEAVY SOUND FESTIVAL 81

LIMITED EDITION

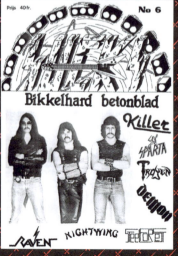

Prijs 40 fr.   No 6

Bikkelhard betonblad

Killer
SPARTA
TROJEN
DEMON

RAVEN   NIGHTWING   Teedorset

NO 8   40 FR.
                    2,5 FL.

ACCEPT
PICTURE
METALLICA
ACID
MOTORHEAD
SAVAGE
VICTIM
THUNDER FIRE
RAVEN
BLACK ROSE

ORKAAN
JAARGANG 1 NR. 2
FEBRUARI '83

ACID
KILLER
TROJAN
SAVAGE
LEGEND
CROSS
FIRE
HAWAII
ACCEPT

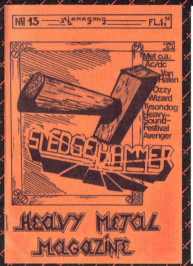

№ 13   3ⁿ jaargang   FL,1,⁵⁰

Met o.a.:
Ac/dc
Van
Halen
Ozzy
Wizard
Tysondog
Heavy–
Sound–
Festival
Avenger

SLEDGEHAMMER

HEAVY METAL Magazine

Suck

MET O.A.   LP-NIEUWS
KILLER
MSG

EN

prijs : 35

ANVIL

EARTHQUAKE '83
HEAVY SOUNDFESTIVAL
AARDSCHOKDAG

Prijs: 60 Fr. of 3.5 Fl.   Nr. 11

Prijs: 35 f   KRIMINEEL   HARDROCKBLAD   No 1

METAL PAPER

HEADBANGER
F 2,50 BFR 45   NO. 5
90¢ 55P DM 2,25

HEAVY SOUND
FESTIVAL '83   VANDENBERG
SPECIAL

MET O.A.: IRON MAIDEN, JAGUAR,
BLACKFOOT, ANVIL L.P.'s
SAXON   FRANK MARINO
ROCK EXPLOSION '83
U.S. METAL (DL.2)

POPERINGE (B) MAECKEBLYDE

ZATERDAG SAMEDI   **23 APRIL AVRIL** — **20 uh**

ENIG CONCERT IN BELGIË
CONCERT EXCEPTIONNEL POUR LA BELGIQUE

FRANK MARINO
&
MAHOGANY RUSH
TREASON

VOORVERKOOP : 320 BF   KASSA   : 360 BF   PRÉVENTE : 50 FF   ENTRÉE : 55 FF

AALTER, Music House
ANTWERPEN, Blue Cheer
BLANKENBERGE, VROB
BRUGGE, Bilbo - Flemisch Record Store - Music Main
DADIZELE, De Nieuwe Smis
DEINZE, The Wave
DIKSMUIDE, 't Kabareke - Freedom Pub
GENT, Bilbo - Music Man
HOUTHULST, Damberd
IEPER, Happy Days
IZEGEM, Elpee Shop

KOEKELARE, Non Stop - Skoe Bidoe
KORTEMARK, Sing Song
KORTRIJK, Popcorner - Ad Fundum - Chopper
LICHTERVELDE, 't Schild
MENEN, Kimson
NIEUWPOORT, Disco-Bar
OOSTENDE, Platencentrum - Barbe Q - Rainbow
POPERINGE, Ghybe - Keikop - Hoppebel - Ons Huis
ROESELARE, Piet Gein
TIELT, De Msebel - Geert Coffez, Stationstraat 16
TORHOUT, Bufalo
VEURNE, The Corner

VLAMERTINGE, Barroo
WAREGEM, De Klub
WERVIK, Les Copains
WEVELGEM, Muziek Soetlok
ARMENTIERES, Studio Penez
BAILLEUL, Electricité J.M. Bouve
DUNKERQUE, Et. G. Rouvroy & Fils
LILLE, Le FNAC - Popson
DOUAI, Moog
LENS, Paris K 7

Telefonische reservaties : 051/58 08 48

Jeugdcafé AD FUNDUM
Langebrugstraat 15, 8500 KORTRIJK
Koninklijke baan 16, 8470 DE PANNE
056/22 19 57

GEERT BEERNAERT
muziekinstrumenten

I used to give each band member and their manager a glass with the name of the band and the venue etched on it. And when it came to the rider, we made sure to stick to it like glue. I remember Frank Marino & Mahogany Rush demanding a couch in the dressing room. And Herman Schueremans tried to pull a fast one on us, claiming they also wanted a... ahem... 'female companion'. It turned out to be just a lame joke. Luc Waeyaert

---

Ticket (yellow):
POPERINGE - MAECKEBLYDE
Zondag 6 februari '83 - 20 uur
UFO
+ SPIDER
Voorverkoop : 320 fr.   Kassa : 360 fr.
Muziekkroeg De Keikop bij Utten
Veurnestraat, Poperinge

Ticket (green):
POPERINGE (B) - MAECKEBLYDE
Zondag 3 april '83 - 20 u.
Dimanche 3 avril '83 - 20 h.
FAREWELL TOUR
ACCEPT
+ SAVAGE
Voorverkoop : 280 Bfr.   Kassa : 340 Bfr.
Prévente : 45 FF   Entrée : 50 FF
Rock-café PIET GEIN Roeselare
Niet geldig zonder strook / Pas valable sans bande   N° 0087

Ticket:
POPERINGE (B.) - MAECKEBLYDE
Zaterdag 23 april '83 - 20 uur
Samedi 23 avril '83 - 20 h.
Enig concert in België.   Concert exceptionnel pour la Belgique
FRANK MARINO & MAHOGANY RUSH   + TREASON
Voorverkoop : 320 Fr.   Kassa : 360 Fr.
Prévente : 50 FF.   Entrée : 55 FF.
ATLETIEK CENTRUM   ONTMOETINGSCENTRUM
ADONIS   ONS HUIS bij Gerard
Ieperstraat 11 - 8970 Poperinga
Tel. 057/33 57 30
Niet geldig zonder strook / Pas valable sans bande   N° 0295

Ticket:
POPERINGE - MAECKEBLYDE
Zaterdag 17 februari '83 - 20 uur
DEF LEPPARD
+ OSTROGOTH
Voorverkoop : 320 fr.   Kassa : 360 fr.
N.V. Vermeersch - Deconinck
Amerikaanse Stockhuizen
Edewallestraat 96   8120 Kortemark

POPERINGE (B) MAECKEBLIJDE

ZONDAG / DIMANCHE 3 APRIL 83 - 20.00 u

FAREWELL TOUR

ACCEPT

SAVAGE

TICKETS :

POPCENTER

BURG-REYNAERTSTRAAT 10   KORTRIJK   056/21 94 89

HARD AND GOOD

Zonnebeke zaal Petrus

9 April '83 20.30u.

TREASON

+ TTD

tickets 100 F.

kontaktadres

TREASON   jeugdcafé AD FUNDUM
Langebrugstraat 15   056·22 19 57
KORTRIJK

CULT. DOEL

Koekelare (B) - Zuudhove

Zaterdag 22 okt. - 20 u.
Samedi 22 oct. - 20 h.

Kaffee De Sportman presents

VIVA

(Germany)

FEATURING BARBARA SCHENKER

(Sister of Rudolf from THE SCORPIONS and sister of MICHAEL SCHENKER)

WILDFIRE (G.B.)

TICKETS

Kaffee DE SPORTMAN
Statiestraat 7, 8140·Staden

POPERINGE (B) MAECKEBLYDE

ZATERDAG / SAMEDI 19 FEBR. FEVR. 83 20 u h

DEF LEPPARD

Support act : OSTROGOTH

VOORVERKOOP / PREVENTE

ZO **10 JUNI** 84   11-22U

POPERINGE BELGIE

HEAVY SOUND FESTIVAL 2

MOTORHEAD
TW.SISTER

LUISTER NAAR
DE STALEN 10
BRT 2 O.VL.

METALLICA
MANOWAR
MERCYFUL FATE
LITA FORD
FAITHFUL BREATH
H.BOMB

FOR THE FIRST TIME ON THE CONTINENT:
MOTORHEAD WITH NEW LINE UP

SPECIAL GUEST:
FESTIVAL DJ MARTIN BAL (ENGELAND)

IF IT AIN'T HEAVY
IT AIN'T ON
MAUSOLEUM

MAUSOLEUM RECORDS ARE
DISTRIBUTED IN BELGIUM
BY INDISC

**JOEPIE
BETONMOLEN**

J-CARD CONNECTION

BAC

MUSIC MAN

RECORD SHOPS
BRUGGE - GENT

✝✝✝✝

Heavy Sound Festival 1984

Things are really coming together at the second round of Heavy Sound. The army of volunteers is firing on all cylinders, the lineup is stacked with heavy metal legends, and the sun is blazing down on the festival grounds like it's got something to prove. For this edition, they move the party from Bruges to Poperinge. And with a lineup even heavier than last year's, this second edition is staking its claim as Europe's first full-blown heavy metal festival.

After the success of the first edition, organisers and fans wanted more. However, the good folks in Bruges weren't too keen on all that noise pollution from last time, so they pulled the plug. But the organisers wouldn't back down from a challenge. So they packed up their amps and headed straight for Poperinge, the holy ground of guitar mayhem in the Westhoek. The perfect spot was recommended by New Abasti Concerts - Luc Waeyaert, Rik Stael and Jean-Pierre Staelen - and this time the alliance would go deeper. From now on, the Abasti crew would be a full part of Heavy Sound.

Now, setting up in Poperinge was no walk in the park. An entire festival had to be created from scratch. It was a different level of work than the previous edition in the old stadium of Cercle Brugge. The organisers had to rely on a trusty network of volunteers, who rolled up their sleeves and brought their own tools—wheelbarrows, hammers, spanners, you name it. And forget about catering for the crew. But did people complain? Not a chance. That's how the metal spirit was back then. It was a Herculean effort, but against all odds, they pulled it off. But we doubt if Mr Moore would've dared to step on stage.

Thanks to the Maeke-Blyde, Poperinge was already a landmark on the map of Western Metallic Europe. But the locals weren't exactly lining up for those gigs. When word got out that Heavy Sound got a festival license for the Don Bosco sports grounds, people started freaking out. A bunch of metalheads unleashed in wide-open fields instead of confined to four walls? People were worried about the noise pollution, the troublemaking and hellraising. But mayor Marc Mahieu wasn't sweating it. Alongside cultural councillor Werner Claeys, he pushed for the festival and made sure they got the green light. The city and the Don Bosco non-profit organisation raked in a pretty penny too: 120,000 Belgian francs up front plus 500,000 francs as insurance. Talk about a win-win.

Back in the day, the locals didn't know what metal was. We're talking about a time before everyone was glued to their screens 24/7. So when Heavy Sound rolled into town, it was like a bomb had gone off. Sure, people heard rumors about rowdy bikers and supposed Satanist rebels, but they had no clue what the metal scene was really about. Pubs and shops went into lockdown mode, boarding up their windows like a storm was coming. The brave few who kept their doors open hit the jackpot. With fans flooding the streets, hoarding beer became the official sport of the day. Heavy Sound shattered records. After the event, figures from Stella Artois revealed that fans had knocked back a whopping 12 pints each. Once they saw the cash rolling in, shrewd shop owners wasted no time taking down their barricades.

The organisers had made tight arrangements with the security services,

↓↓↓↓↓↓↓↓↓↓↓↓↓

We're talking about a time before everyone was glued to their screens 24/7. So when Heavy Sound rolled into town, it was like a bomb went off. Sure, people heard rumors about rowdy bikers and supposed Satanist rebels, but they had no clue what the metal scene was really about.

↓↓↓↓↓↓↓↓↓↓↓↓↓

but had underestimated one thing: Heavy Sound decided to open a free camping area for all the die-hard fans trekking to Poperinge from miles around. What they had not anticipated was that the fans would arrive two days in advance. So, come Friday evening, the campsite was already buzzing with activity. But with nothing happening on the main stage until Saturday, fans decided to hit the town center for some pre-game action. Problem was, most of the pubs had battened down the hatches as a precaution. In those pubs that did open, there were a few scuffles, especially when some of them started banning leather jackets. As tempers flared, some windows got smashed. But in the grand scheme of things, it was nothing more than a just few minor brawls.

Worse was when some fools mucked about with the gravestones in a military cemetery nearby. Singing songs about the devil is one thing, but messing with war graves? That's just not cool. The organisers were totally bummed out by what happened and made it clear they were not okay with it. It seemed like it could've been the end of the festival, but luckily, that didn't happen. Although it later turned out to be prophetic.

Saturday night's shenanigans set the tone for a tense start of the actual festival day. They had to bring in about a hundred extra cops from Ghent, ready with tear gas just in case. But despite all that, the vibe between the organisers, the city, and the police seemed to be chill, according to the reporters on the scene. The security folks played it cool too, not overdoing it, just keep-

ing a watchful eye while they let the party roll on. Heavy Sound had their private security crew patrolling the grounds as well, so everything went smoothly without a hitch.

The media, fans, and fanzines all raved about the festival lineup for the day, and the sound was on point for most of the time, which was a step up from last year. The plan was to kick things off with a 'festival mass' at 10 in the morning, since it was Pentecost weekend. But seeing those leather jackets with 'Highway To Hell' written on them on Saturday afternoon disturbed the local priest so he bailed out. The real fun started around 11 am, with the early birds busting out the traditional French can-can. Shortly after, H-Bomb from France took the stage and got the rock rolling. The German vikings of Faithful Breath didn't really hit it off with the crowd, but Lita Ford - she had been in Poperinge before, with The Runaways in '77 - warmed things up nicely for the main event: Mercyful Fate from Denmark. It was their first time in Belgium, but they were on fire! People are still talking about the insane talent of the musicians, King Diamond's killer vocals, and the whole satanic spectacle complete with skulls, crossbones, and face paint.

The organisers had initially planned not to rebook any acts, but then Manowar cancelled, leaving them scrambling for a replacement. Some say Manowar was holed up in the studio, while others claim it was some kind of dispute with their management. Whatever the deal, they brought in Baron Rojo again, the Spanish sensation from last year. Once again, their set was dripping with energy, setting the stage for Metallica to unleash their young metal attack. These guys would really click with Poperinge, playing three gigs there in '84, which totally earns them a separate chapter further on in this book.

After Metallica's raging thrash metal set, Twisted Sister rolled in with their colourful, classic NYC-style heavy metal. Their highly popular 'Stay Hungry' album topped the charts in the US, but got mixed reactions from their die-hard fans. Bigmouthed frontman Dee Snider totally owned the stage, hyping up the crowd with rage and getting them all pumped. Motörhead to closed out the night. The organisers personally picked them up at Zaventem airport, where Lemmy, the notorious Jack D fanatic, was already down to the bottom of his first bottle. But

All in all, metal history was written at Heavy Sound in 1984. The crowd enjoyed the killer lineup, and technical glitches were kept to a minimum.

that didn't stop them from delivering a tight show, thanks in part to their own gear that no other band was allowed to touch.

All in all, metal history was written at Heavy Sound in 1984. The crowd enjoyed the killer lineup, and technical glitches were kept to a minimum. Sure, it freaked out a few locals, even though most people agreed the crowd was mostly chill young folk having a good time. After 4pm, they even let local residents in for free, but still, some were on edge. And you know how it goes, the local politicians were all over it, trying to score some points. In the end the organisers were left with a sour taste in their mouths, considering they had invested roughly seven million francs in the event. It was a serious gamble, but it wasn't going to stop them from aiming for a third round.

The next day, while cleaning up, we collected the rubbish from the dressing rooms. It was mostly fruit, but we had no clue what to do with it. So, I took it out to the parking lot, piled it up, splashed some petrol on it, and lit it up. Boom! Instant explosion, and suddenly I'm heading home looking like a mummy, with bandages all over. At least my eyes and nose were still doing their thing. *Rik Stael*

⸸⸸⸸⸸⸸⸸⸸⸸⸸⸸⸸⸸

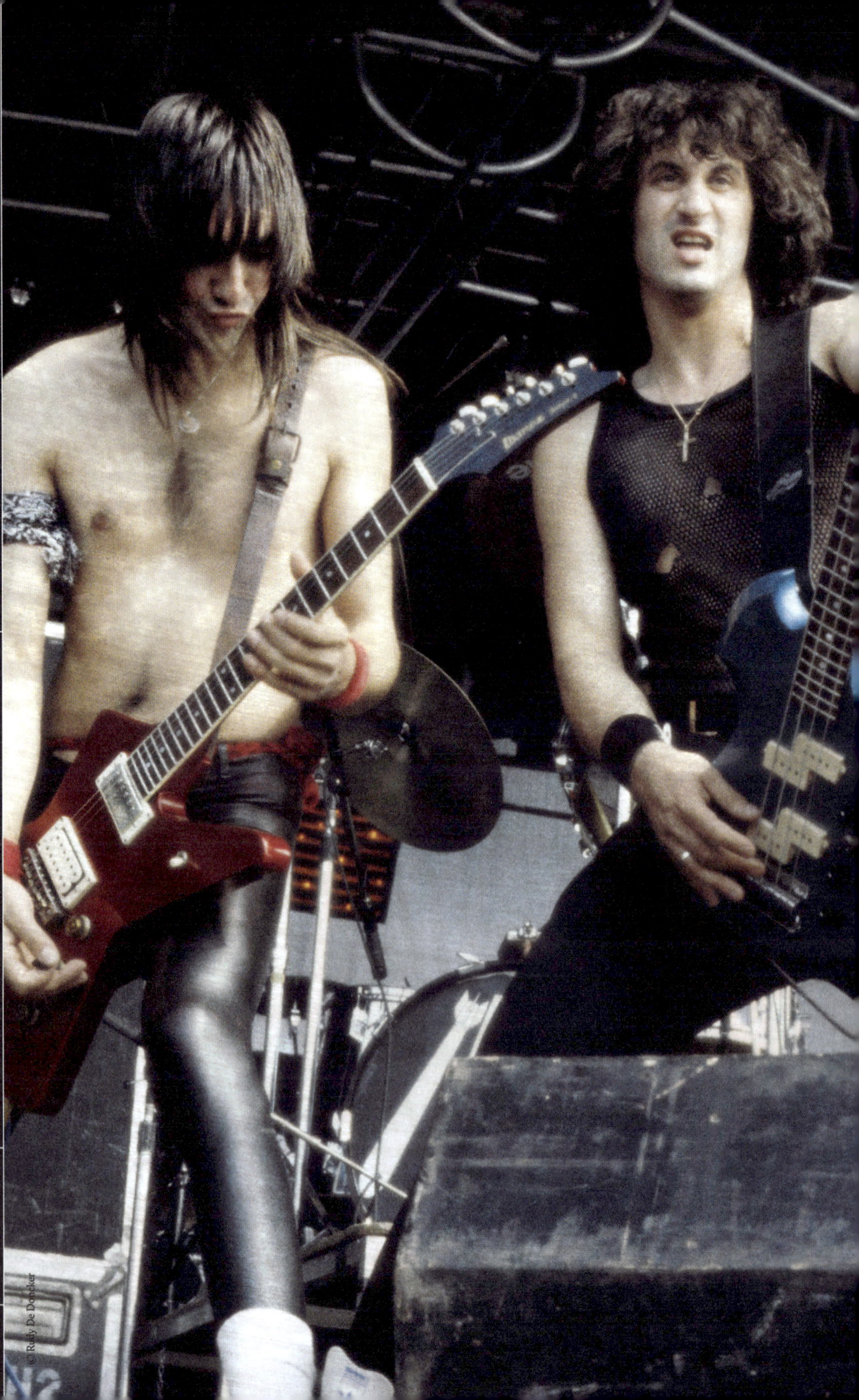

© Rudy De Doncker

Last weekend, Heavy Sound festival was the talk of Poperinge. Opinions were mixed, but you've probably heard that already. What you might not have heard is the crazy story about two young kids from Limburg. On Friday morning, these two 13-year-olds were supposed to be heading to school, or at least that's what their folks thought. But as soon as they stepped out the door, they ditched their backpacks and hopped on a train to Poperinge. When they didn't show up at home that night, their parents got worried. They searched their rooms and found flyers for the Heavy Sound Festival, which was a dead giveaway. So, they called the police in Poperinge, who found the duo at the festival rocking the classic jeans and metal gear. The boys had to empty their pockets, and one of them even had 20,000 Belgian francs (roughly 500 euros) stashed away. Which made the jaws of the lawmen drop. "And I've already blown 10,000," one of them admitted. They had taken 30,000 francs from home, just to be prepared for anything they could encounter on an adventure like this. They had even shopped for some cool-looking stonewashed jeans. A few hours later, their folks swooped in to pick them up, probably with a mix of relief and "What the @&xxx! were you thinking, son?" vibes. *Excerpt from an article in Op St-Bertens*

✟✟✟✟✟✟✟✟✟✟✟✟✟

Faithful Breath must have sweated
like pigs in their Viking gear that day.
It was so bloody hot.

Murf Hille

✟✟✟✟✟✟✟✟✟✟✟✟✟

Lita Ford

© PG Brunelli

✝✝✝✝✝✝✝✝✝✝✝✝

At noon, H-Bomb from France kicked things off with a casual "Good evening, Poperinge!" Then we saw the Vikings of Faithful Breath sorely miss the mark, followed by King Diamond, whose makeup was starting to run. Lita Ford rocked the stage (and a pair of leather pants), and Twisted Sister totally nailed it with a powerful set. What a festival!

Barda Truc

✝✝✝✝✝✝✝✝✝✝✝✝

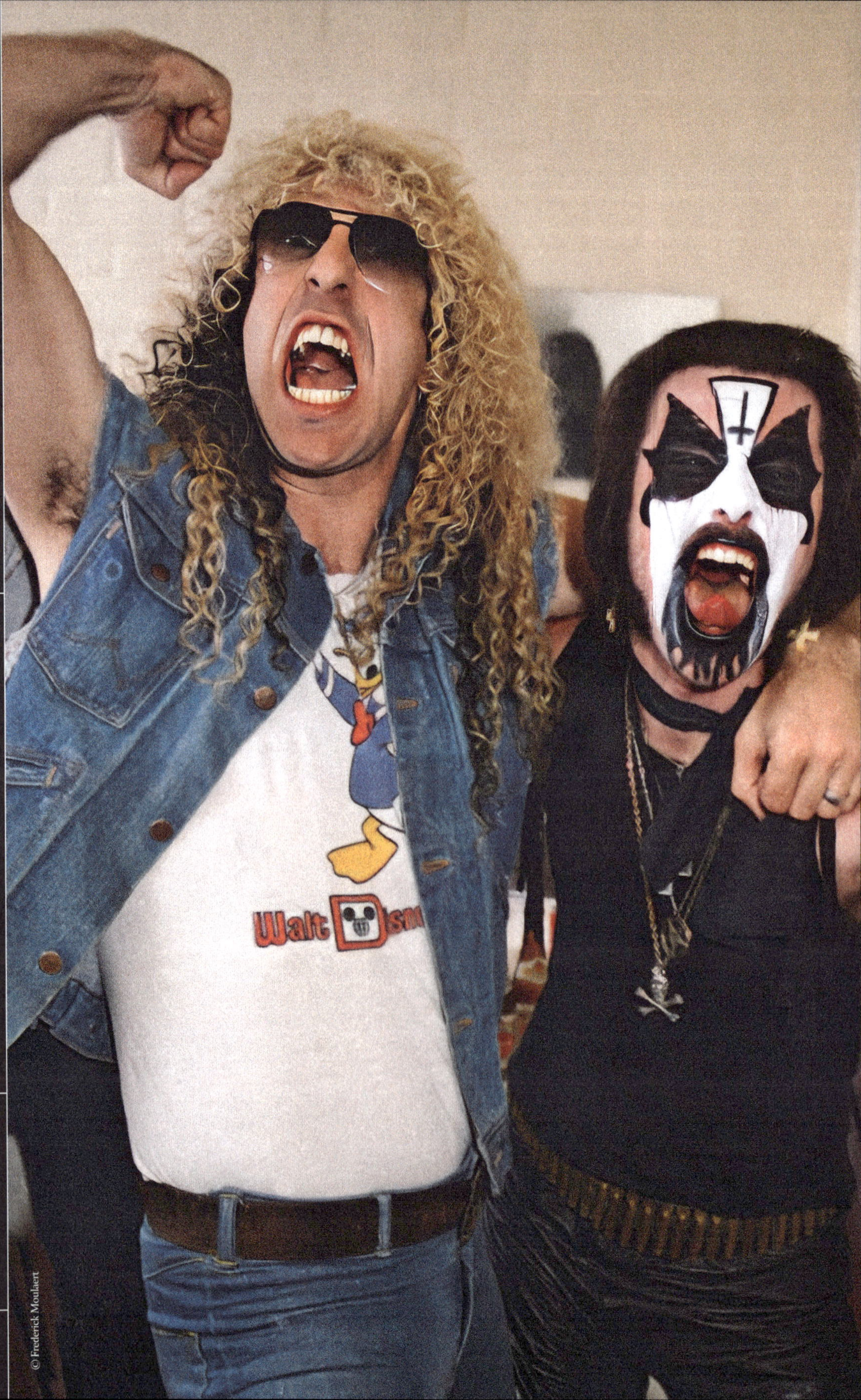

10-06-1984

Heavy Sound Festival '84 - Poperinge

Mercyful Fate

For Mercyful Fate, Heavy Sound was an unforgettable experience. Sharing the stage with bands like Baron Rojo, Twisted Sister, and Metallica was epic. I even kept the old pale yellow backstage pass as a souvenir. Can you believe it was just a basic photocopy? No fancy laminated passes back then! But that gig was a game-changer for Mercyful Fate. They really kicked it up a notch after that. *Ole Bang, Mercyful Fate manager*

When my mum married my stepdad, he was well-known in our hometown of Kortrijk and totally obsessed with hard rock. His house was like a shrine to vinyl. One day in '84, I was flipping through his impressive collection — Budgie, Deep Purple, KISS, you name it — when Mercyful Fate's debut album caught my eye. Turns out, my stepdad and Jacques from the Popcenter record shop were friends. They even hopped on a boat to London once and met King Diamond during a Mercyful Fate promo tour for the 'Melissa' LP. My stepdad snapped up that record and holy hell, it blew me away! 'Black Funeral' became my anthem, probably because it was my first taste of their wicked sound and those insane high-pitched vocals. And don't even get me started on the devilish artwork—I was hooked. The cover even had a shoutout written on it: "To Johan the weekend warrior, rock on." King clearly didn't know my stepdad was a 24-hour party animal. Later on, he gave me that record as a present. And every Christmas and birthday I stacked up my Mercyful Fate/King Diamond collection. One thing is for sure: I'll never part with that first record. *Hans Verbeke*

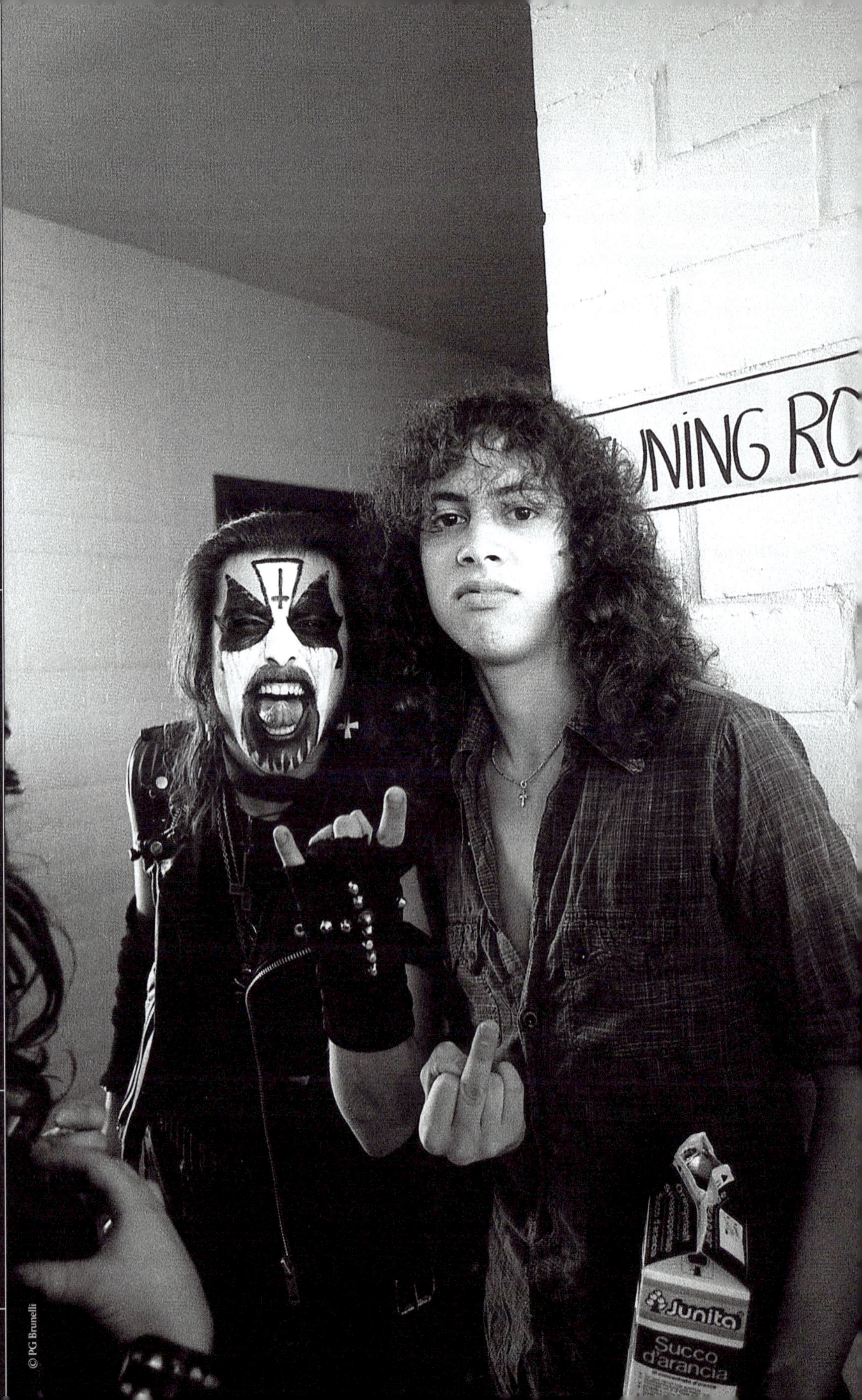

Mercyful Fate

Heavy Sound Festival '84 - Poperinge

10-06-1984

© PG Brunelli

✝✝✝✝✝✝✝✝✝✝✝✝✝

I can still picture it like it was yesterday.
King Diamond giving Hank Shermann the evil eye for
his stage outfit. I mean, the guy looked like he rolled
out of bed and straight onto the stage, sporting baggy
sweatpants and a plain white t-shirt.

André 'Aardschok' Verhuysen

✝✝✝✝✝✝✝✝✝✝✝✝✝

King Diamond

The Filthy Fifteen

Back in the early '80s, Mercyful Fate were pushing boundaries and seriously stirring up the establishment. King Diamond, their frontman, wasn't shy about promoting his ties to the Church of Satan, thanks to Anton LaVey. But alongside all that controversy, Mercyful Fate brought something totally fresh and different to the scene. Their tunes were packed with intricate riffs, killer hooks, and King's psychotic falsetto vocals. It wasn't until later that people really started to appreciate their groundbreaking sound, turning them into the legendary cult band they are today.

The band's devilish vibe often led to their gigs being cancelled. Back in the '80s, there was this massive anti-satanism crusade sweeping the USA. It was like the Great Horned One was getting blamed for every bad thing under the sun, and people were ready to grab their pitchforks at the drop of a hat. From drug and child abuse to murder and violence, the finger was pointed at Satanists for it all. And with Ronald Reagan's conservative party in charge, the whole thing got blown up on TV, stirring up a frenzy. That's when the super strict Parents Music Resource Center (PMRC) came into play in '84, spending the next decade kicking up a fuss about dodgy lyrics, especially in heavy metal songs.

Guitarist Michael Denner recalls: "1984 was a great year for Mercyful Fate. We were gigging like crazy, and with King's occult and satanic persona, we were already making waves. Then out of the blue, we got this unexpected promo boost from Tipper Gore and her PMRC in the US. They were the ones pushing for those parental warning stickers on albums with so-called adult content. The PMRC released 'The Filthy Fifteen', a list of tracks they thought were morally corrupt and should be kept away from kids. And guess what? We found ourselves rubbing shoulders with the likes of AC/DC, Venom, Mötley Crüe and evil witches like Sheena Easton and Cyndi Lauper on that list."

"In terms of publicity, it was like hitting the jackpot. The PMRC were totally clueless, and they ended up getting roasted for that later on. I mean, they even had a congressional hearing where rockers like Dee Snider from Twisted Sister made them look ridiculous. All the other artists on that list were mega stars. Next thing you know, we're being mentioned alongside the likes of Madonna and Prince. You can't put a price on that kind of exposure."

King Diamond's lyrics weren't exactly aimed at the Sunday choir crowd. King was a full-on Satanist who wasn't shy about ruffling some feathers with Christian hardliners. When a priest accused him of leading youngsters down the left hand path with his track 'A Dangerous Meeting', King didn't back down. He countered them, stating it was more like a caution sign you'd see at a building site—a heads-up rather than an invitation.

╫╫╫╫╫╫╫╫╫╫╫╫

The PMRC put out 'The Filthy Fifteen', a list of songs
they thought were morally corrupted and that parents
needed to keep an eye on.

╫╫╫╫╫╫╫╫╫╫╫╫

© Frederiek Moulaert

✝✝✝✝✝✝✝✝✝✝✝✝✝

The second edition had some heavy hitters that would soon become household
names: Metallica, Motörhead, and Mercyful Fate were all smashing it. Metallica was just starting to make ripples, but they already had a solid fanbase.
Manowar was supposed to play too, but they pulled out last minute. We had
some dispute with their agency that we couldn't shake off. Guess that's why
they didn't make it. You know how it is in that scene—money talks, but for
us, it was all about having fun. *Luc Waeyaert, written by Stefan Carlier*

✝✝✝✝✝✝✝✝✝✝✝✝✝

† † † † † † † † † † † † †

Can you believe it's been 40 years since Twisted Sister first whipped up a storm on Belgian turf? Back in '84, they played the epic Heavy Sound Festival in Poperinge, squeezed in between Metallica and Motörhead. 'Stay Hungry' had only dropped a few months prior, and already went triple platinum in the States alone, selling around 3 million copies. Europe has always shown them love, but that first gig at Heavy Sound Festival? They'll never forget that killer lineup and the warm welcome they got. *Pete Sanders*

† † † † † † † † † † † † †

© PG Brunelli

Heavy Sound Festival '84 - Poperinge

Twisted Sister

© Rudy De Doncker

✝✝✝✝✝✝✝✝✝✝✝✝

That festival happened right at the
peak of the golden heavy metal
years! I'll always remember
Dee Snider mouthing off the back
rows for not getting involved.
After his verbal outburst,
the whole crowd just went
completely nuts!

Barda Truc

✝✝✝✝✝✝✝✝✝✝✝✝

Twisted Sister

Heavy Sound Festival '84 - Poperinge

10-06-1984

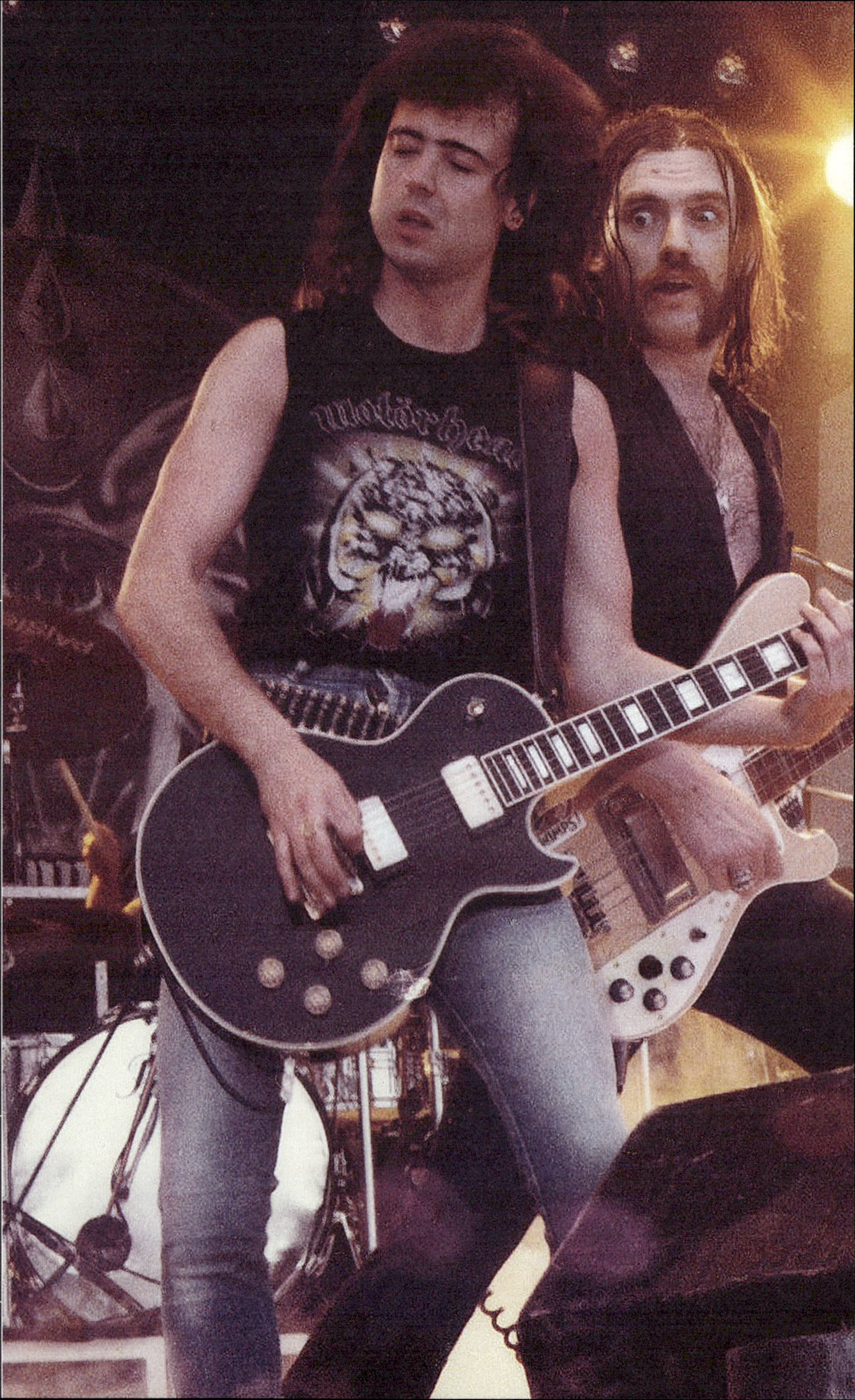

Motörhead

Heavy Sound Festival '84 - Poperinge

10-06-1984

© Joseph Carducci

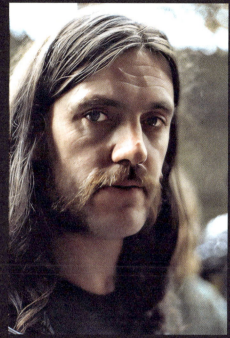

✝✝✝✝✝✝✝✝✝✝✝✝✝

Every contract comes with a rider that mentions the artists' food and drink demands. For some bands, that included specific types of exotic smoking herbs. Herman Schueremans once tipped me off about a band that demanded 'sweets'. We ended up stocking up on a bunch of kiddie treats because, hey, who knew, right? I drove Lemmy from Motörhead to the airport that year. He was barely awake and was already down to the bottom of his first bottle of Jack.
Luc Waeyaert

✝✝✝✝✝✝✝✝✝✝✝✝✝

© Westhoek verbeeldt, privécollectie

Our long journey from Limburg to Poperinge by bus was a right laugh. It didn't take more than 30 minutes before we'd guzzled all the beer onboard, leading to a quickfire round of pee stops. When we finally arrived at the festival ground, it all looked a bit amateurish, but as it turned out, they had their act together. Security was tight, courtesy of the Outlaws, a notorious biker gang back then. I'll never forget that parked car blocking part of the entrance. After a few announcements on the mic, the owner still didn't show up. The Outlaws took it apart, bit by bit, and stacked up the parts in a tent. Classic! Wish I could've seen the look on the owner's face when he came to pick up his car. *Danny Vandevelde*

On that early train ride from Antwerp to Poperinge, my mates and I were already quite pissed. I decided to test my smoking skills by seeing if I could puff through my ear by sucking my cigarette real hard. Next thing I knew, someone dumped a pint of beer on my head because my hair was literally on fire... There I was, with a scorched scalp and an earful of blisters! Ended up at the doctor's, who was flat out busy, of course. Ah well, you live and you learn, right? *Frederic Washal*

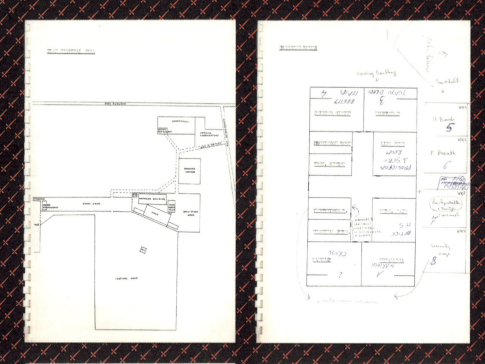

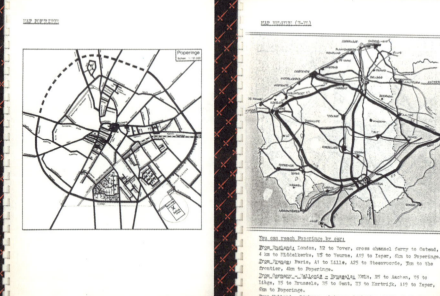

You can reach Poperinge by car:

From England: London, M2 to Dover, cross channel ferry to Ostend, 4 km to Middelkerke, N5 to Veurne, A19 to Ieper, 6km to Poperinge.
From France: Paris, A1 to Lille, A25 to Steenvoorde, 7km to the frontier, 4km to Poperinge.
From Germany - Wallonia - Brussels: Köln, N5 to Aachen, N5 to Liège, N5 to Brussels, N5 to Gent, N3 to Kortrijk, A19 to Ieper, 6km to Poperinge.
From Holland - Limburg - Antwerp: Amsterdam, N10 to Rotterdam, N10 to Breda, N10 to Antwerp, N3 to Gent, N3 to Kortrijk, A19 to Ieper, 6km to Poperinge.

From the very beginning, the Heavy Sound festival aimed at an international audience. As Poperinge is not exactly Metropolis, the promotion team distributed flyers with a map of Belgium and detailed directions for visitors from all over the world.

BETALING GROEPEN

GROEPEN	VALUTA	6 APRIL	20 APRIL	27 APRIL	1 MEI	18 MEI	10 JUNI	TOTAAL
MOTORHEAD	5000 £	/	/	190 000	/	190000	/	
TWISTED SISTER	4500 £	. /	174.280	/	177000	/	/	
METALLICA	3800 £	146.743	/	/	150 000	/	/	
MANOWAR	3500 £	/	/	/	220 000	/	/	
MERCY FATE	30000 DM	/	/	.	85 000	/	85000	
LITA FORD	2000 £	77.316	/	/	80 000	. /	/	
FAITH F. BREATH	1250 DM	/	/	/	/	/	25 000	
H. BOMB	4000 FF	/	/	/	/	/	25.000	
TOTAAL	/	224.109	174 280					

DE NIEUWE AARDSCHOK

KEIHARD ROCKBLAD...VERSCHIJNT MAANDELIJKS
PRIJS: FL.4,50..BF:90

Lita Ford in Paradiso
**Heavy Sound Festival
Dio op Pinkpop
Iron Maiden part 3
Sortilège**

NR. 15/ JULI '84

50bf
nr 2

HARD HEAVY

interview:
VENOM
DIO
ACID
Y & T
H BOMB

en ook nog: Black Widow, Killer,
Pretty Maids, Overdrive, Jaguar.

TYMPANS
ROCK - PRESS

N°1   AVRIL MAI '84   43 FB 7 FF

VENUM

le hard en wallonie
l'alternatif en Europe

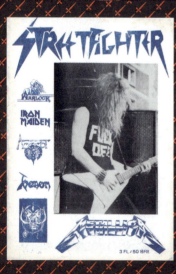

STREETFIGHTER

WARLOCK
IRON MAIDEN
ACCEPT
VENOM

3 FL / 50 BFR

NR 1 WHIPLASH
Hard Rock & Heavy Metal Magazine
45 FR. 2,5 FL.

SEPTEMBER - OKTOBER 1984

INTERVIEUWS:	VERDER NOG:
MOTORHEAD	HEAVY SOUND FESTIVAL
SAVAGE	PANDEMONIUM
CULPRIT	ARTILLERY
TYSONDOG	AARDSCHOKDAG
BLACK WIDOW	GILGAMESJ E.A.

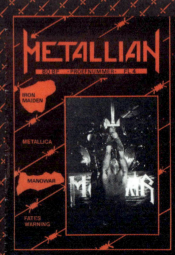

METALLIAN
80 BF PROEFNUMMER FL.4

IRON MAIDEN

METALLICA

MANOWAR

FATES WARNING

236

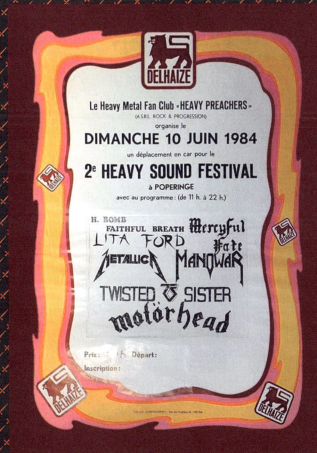

Coaches for the Heavy Sound festival were booked from far and wide. The Brussels heavy metal fan club 'Heavy Preachers' even cobbled together their own poster with the help of a local supermarket.

12-02-1984

Maeke-Blyde - Poperinge

Venom

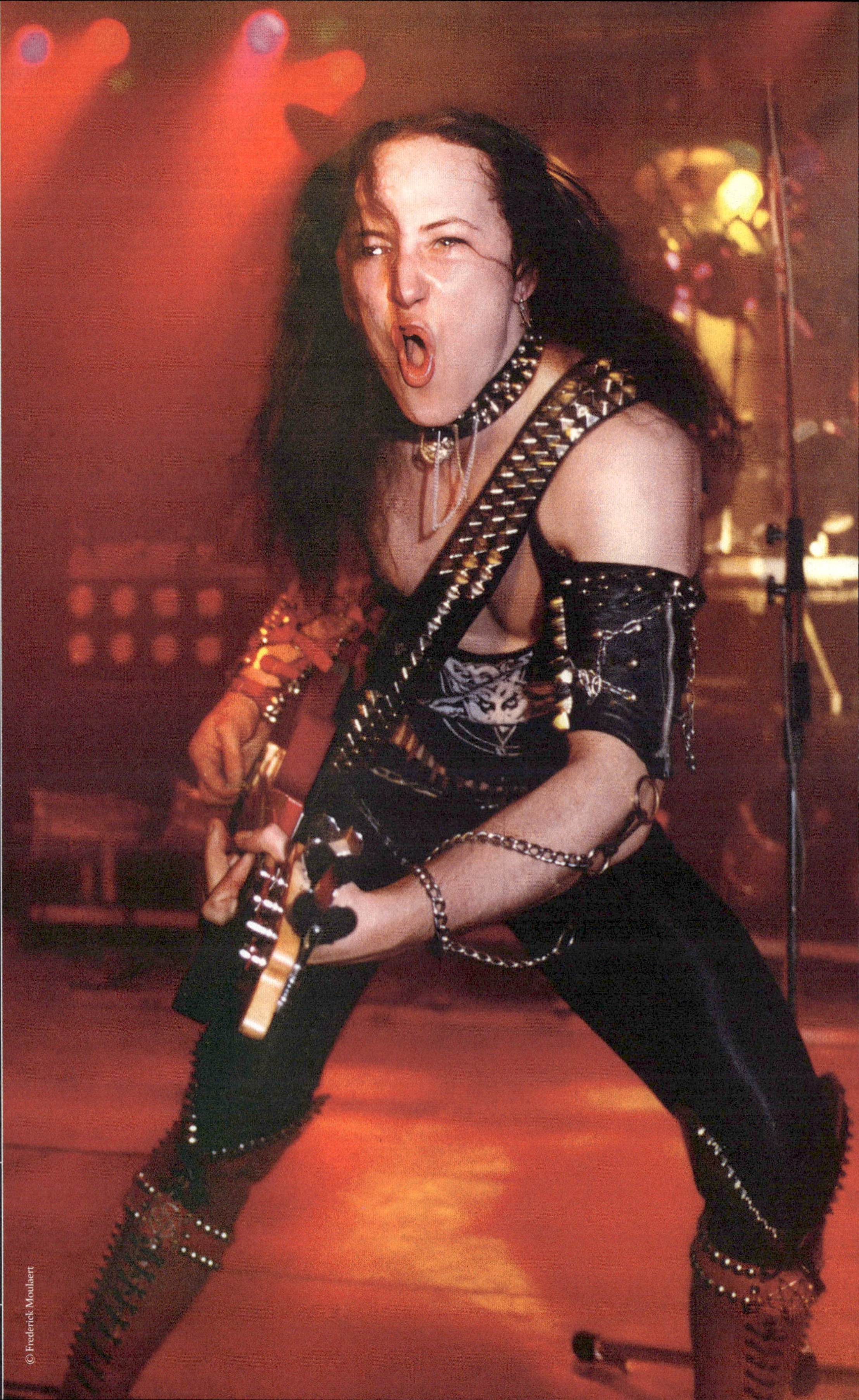
© Frederick Moulaert

Back in '84, Venom were riding high on their metal throne. They were the originators of extreme metal, boasting a massive following on both sides of the pond. What started as aversion turned into global fame, but it wasn't all smooth sailing for an unconventional metal band. On one side, you had the classic heavy metal bands like Maiden, Priest, and Manowar. And then there was this fresh thrash metal scene emerging, thanks in part to Venom's influence. But in those early days, even Iron Maiden was deemed too extreme for some folks. Venom found themselves at a major crossroads. The trio could've gone either way, but they stubbornly stuck to their guns. *Metal A Review*

Maeke-Blyde - Poperinge

Venom

✝✝✝✝✝✝✝✝✝✝✝✝✝

Black is the night, metal we fight
Power amps set to explode
Energy screams, magic and dreams
Satan records their first note
We chime the bell, chaos in Hell
Metal for maniacs pure
Fast-melting steel, fortune on wheels
Brain hemorrhage is the cure
Lay down your soul to the gods rock 'n' roll

Black Metal, 1982

✝✝✝✝✝✝✝✝✝✝✝✝✝

EMI RECORDS (UK)
20 MANCHESTER SQUARE LONDON W1A 1ES
TELEPHONE 01-486 4488
TELEX 22643
CABLES EMIRECORD LONDON W1

Dear Venom,

```
FFFFFFFFFFF      UU        UU    CCCCCCCCC    KK        KK
FFFFFFFFFFF      UU        UU    CCCCCCCCC    KK        KK
FF               UU        UU    CC           KK    KK
FFFFFF           UU        UU    CC           KK  KK
FFFFFF           UU        UU    CC           KKKK
FF               UU        UU    CC           KK  KK
FF               UU        UU    CC           KK    KK
FF               UUUUUUUUUU      CCCCCCCCC     KK        KK
FF               UUUUUUUUUU      CCCCCCCCC     KK        KK
```

```
OOOOO OOOOO      FFFFFFFFFFF     FFFFFFFFFFF
OOOOO OOOOO      FFFFFFFFFFF     FFFFFFFFFFF
OO       OO      FF              FF
OO       OO      FFFFFF          FFFFFF
OO       OO      FFFFFF          FFFFFF
OO       OO      FF              FF
OO       OO      FF              FF
OOOOO OOOOO      FF              FF
OOOOO OOOOO      FF              FF
```

WITH COMPLIMENTS

THE GREATEST MUSIC COMPANY IN THE WORLD

EMI RECORDS LIMITED REGISTERED OFFICE: BLYTH ROAD, HAYES, MIDDLESEX. REGISTERED IN ENGLAND, NO. 68172

A THORN EMI COMPANY

As always, the music business was a bit slow catching on to the latest trends, as shown by this polite "thanks, but no thanks" given to Venom.

Poperinge (B) MAECKEBLIJDE

Dimanche 12 février
Zondag 12 februari 1984   20.00 u

**VENOM
METALLICA**

Tickets : 320 - 360

ABASTI
CONCERTS
VZW

BACKSTAGE

PLP Presents

**Friday June 1st 1984 7.30pm
LONDON HAMMERSMITH
ODEON
"Seven Dates of Hell" Tour '84**

venom

Zurich   Paris
Milan   Zwolle
Nuremburg   Poperinge
                  London

Plus   Special Guests

DUMPY'S RUSTY BOLTS

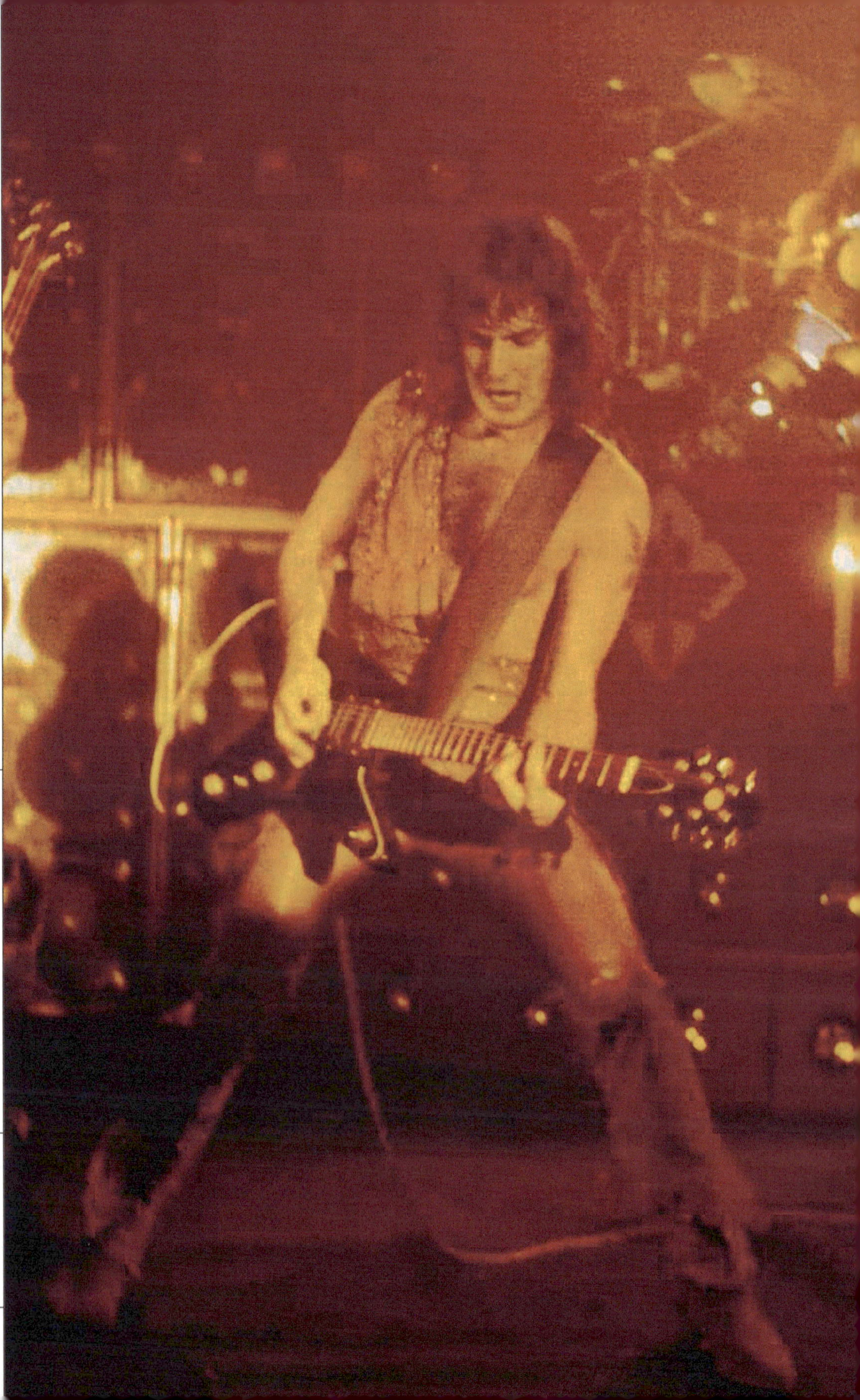

Our songs are raw and merciless,
and our take on the world doesn't hold
back on the cynicism. Heavy metal is
our lifeblood, our calling. Everything
else? Just background noise. Too many
of today's American bands are lame,
playing it safe. But not Manowar.
We go all the way, leaving nothing
but rubble in our wake.

Ross The Boss, Manowar

While American radio kept churning out the same old Foreigner and Journey tunes, the underground heavy metal scene toiled on with perseverance. One of those rebel bands was Manowar, a bunch of leather and fur clad NYC lads who proudly dubbed their music 'Male-Oriented Rock'. With their album 'Sign Of The Hammer' under their studded belts, Manowar shot to stardom and embarked on their first European tour. Now, these guys had a bit of a rep for pulling the plug on gigs, which they did for the 1984 edition of the Heavy Sound festival. But come October 5th of that year, they finally hit Belgium for the first time, invading the stage of the Maeke-Blyde in Poperinge. They brought Belgium's Thunderfire, and Alaska, Bernie Marsden from Whitesnake's new band, in tow.

This is how the Metallian fanzine reported the gig:

"When the New York barbarians hit the stage, they were shrouded in a thick cloud of smoke, making it tricky to even see who was up there. But what really grabbed attention was the fierce, stone-faced look on the band members' faces—not a grin in sight. And just when the whole stage vanished behind a massive smoke screen, the lights cut out and chaos erupted in the crowd. Not surprising, really, after two lacklustre support acts. Then, with a five-minute intro tape setting the scene, Manowar kicked things off with their debut album's title track. And from there, it was full throttle, with 'Blood of My Enemies' sending shockwaves across the stage. They rolled out their new song 'All Men Play on Ten' after 'Secret of Steel', then blasted through classics like 'Metal Daze' and 'Thor (The Powerhead)'. Grandmaster Joey DeMaio took the spotlight next, busting out bass-heavy interludes 'Thunderpick' and 'William's Tale'. The guy is definitely up there with the greats. And let's not forget Scott Columbus, whose thunderous drum solo morphed seamlessly into the killer intro of 'Kill with Power'. As the echoes of 'Die, Die, Die,...' faded away, 'Fast Taker' tore through the venue like a speeding locomotive, whipping the crowd into a frenzy of headbanging madness."

The men of war clearly weren't familiar with the concept of taking a break, because right after 'Warlord', they hit us with another banger, 'I've Sworn the Oath', blasting through the speakers with enough force to knock you sideways. And just when you thought they couldn't crank it up any higher, they unleashed 'Sign Of The Hammer', a warning shot that had us all on edge. Then came the ultimate showdown: a mammoth rendition of 'Battle Hymns', flawlessly executed and cranked up to eleven, like something out of a blockbuster playback show. And to wrap it all up, singer Eric Adams delivered the final blow with a mighty swing of his trusty sword, leaving the crowd breathless and floored. *Gig review from Metallian fanzine*

✝✝✝✝✝✝✝✝✝✝✝✝✝

*Manowar brings
the thunder with real,
unadulterated metal -
no gimmicks,
no smoke and mirrors.
It's pure Manowar,
through and through.*

Joey DeMaio, Manowar

✝✝✝✝✝✝✝✝✝✝✝✝✝

↓↓↓↓↓↓↓↓↓↓↓↓↓

Since a few weeks, these striking red posters have been all over the place, screaming "We are under siege! Your country needs you!" Sounds dramatic, right? Well, apparently, Manowar and its Battalions of Steel are about to invade our hometown Poperinge. They're all set to attack the Maeke-Blyde on October 5th at 8:00pm. Better mark your calendars and get ready for a full-on metal clash!

Fast forward to October 5th, 1984, 7:55 PM. I'm geared up and ready for action, standing my ground alongside the national army. And then, boom! Thunderfire shows up, leading the charge like a battering ram. Sure, they're a bit wild and unpredictable, but they pack a punch, taking out our front lines with blasts of raw energy.

After a short breather to patch up our wounded, Alaska takes the lead for round two. This squad might not have the fanciest gear, but they are technically skilled and master their weaponry. Their combat methods may be a bit outdated, but Alaska proves to be highly effective in its own way.

Then, it's time to call in the cavalry. Killing machine Manowar rolls in with a deafening roar, flattening us with their steamrolling soundwaves. Our troops try to push back, but it's no use, Manowar cannot be stopped. They come at us again, even stronger this time, using smoke, blinding lights and ear-splitting noise as weapons of mass destruction. We stand no chance. Our defences take the final fall as their epic performance goes for the throat, leading them straight to victory. Manowar kills! *Gauthier*

↓↓↓↓↓↓↓↓↓↓↓↓↓

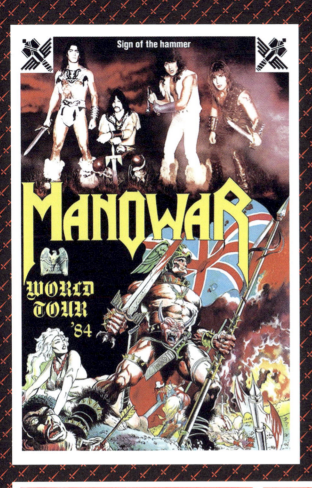

Seek and destroy Belgium

Back in '84, Metallica ripped through Poperinge three times. First time, they were almost there, about to hit it big. But by the third gig, they were totally primed for stardom. Now, looking back, we saw them transform into the ultimate gods of US thrash metal. And the city of hops was all too happy to give them a boost (plus a couple of cold brews)!

Lightning strikes the Westhoek

Metallica burst onto the scene in 1983 with their debut album, 'Kill 'Em All'. Suddenly, metal and punk were like two sides of the same coin. Metallica were the ones who first pulled Excalibur out of the stone. Later dubbed thrash metal, it sparked a whole new movement. Their first gig in Poperinge happened in February '84, opening for the legendary UK band Venom, pioneers of both thrash and black metal.

After their European tour with Venom, Metallica spent a few weeks in Copenhagen, which Lars Ulrich, the de facto leader, called home. They basically camped out at Sweet Silence Studio for a month, recording at night since the daytime slots were fully booked. They caught some sleep during the few daylight hours Denmark offered. They roughed it out in the studio because there was no budget for hotels. Those were some dark, concrete bunker days that seeped into the epic 'Ride the Lightning', a monumental record that still stands tall in the genre. With bassist Cliff Burton on-board, the band explored new song structures, Lars kicked it up a notch with his drum beats, Kirk Hammett shredded his guitar to bits, and James Hetfield elevated it all to godlike levels with his vocals.

This is not the spot for a full-on Metallica bio, plenty of books out there did that already. But let's look at the production quality of 'Ride the Lightning'. Put 'Fight Fire With Fire' up against any other metal track from '84, and you'll feel its impact in your bones. The sheer strength of the songs and the heavy riffs were unprecedented at the time.

After wrapping up in the studio in March, Metallica kept the party going with a European tour. Even before their album hit the shelves, they were back in action at the Heavy Sound Festival in Poperinge. Their last tour had been a blast, and they snagged a prime spot on the bill, right before Twisted Sister. As James Hetfield mentioned in an interview that day they were still fanboys themselves. Just two years ago, they were going nuts over Motörhead in the crowd, and now they were sharing the stage with them. That led to some serious headbanging with the fans and loads of new pals. And since they were too young to drink back home in California, they were all in on Belgium's vivid beer scene.

↓↓↓↓↓↓↓↓↓↓↓↓↓

Put 'Fight Fire With Fire' up against any other metal track from '84, and you'll feel its impact in your bones. The sheer strength of the songs and the heavy riffs were unprecedented at the time.

↓↓↓↓↓↓↓↓↓↓↓↓↓

Pimple-faced legends

'Ride the Lightning' hit the shelves like a bolt of lightning in July 1984. Rave reviews rolled in, and a whole new surge of fans fell head over heels for Metallica. But not everyone went wild about the lightning-fast pace of their music. Some metalheads thought it was ridiculously over the top. But still, the band's fanbase kept on growing.

James Hetfield is a total music freak. And if you need proof, just check out his battlevest. He's got it decked out with patches of punk and metal legends. Even the Belgian band Ostrogoth scores a prime spot.

And guess where the boys from Frisco ended up later that year? Yep, back in Poperinge for the third time. This time they were headlining the Maeke-Blyde and took no prisoners. Tank rolled onto the stage like a metal juggernaut and left the crowd shell-shocked. Then Metallica hit the stage like a nuclear bomb going off. The crowd went absolutely crazy, and the band was right there with them, pump-ing up the energy even more. The roadies tried to keep everyone in check, but it was no use—the fans were unstoppable. Some kids got roughed up in the chaos and had to be carried out, but that didn't stop the show. They played pretty much every song from both albums, and then some. Metallica didn't just come, they conquered—three times over. We witnessed the birth of a legend that year.

© Frederic Montbert

© Frederick Moulaert

The first cut is the deepest

I'm chilling at Café Le Tram in Poperinge with my Brussels buddies Yves Tchao and Didier Sorgeloos, just hanging out at the big central table. Suddenly, in walk Kirk, Cliff, Lars, James, and their tour manager/sound engineer. They spot us and ask if they can join in. James and Kirk are over at the bar, settling the tab, and that's when I snap my very first photo of Metallica. Later, we grab another shot outside the café. *Frederick Moulaert, photographer*

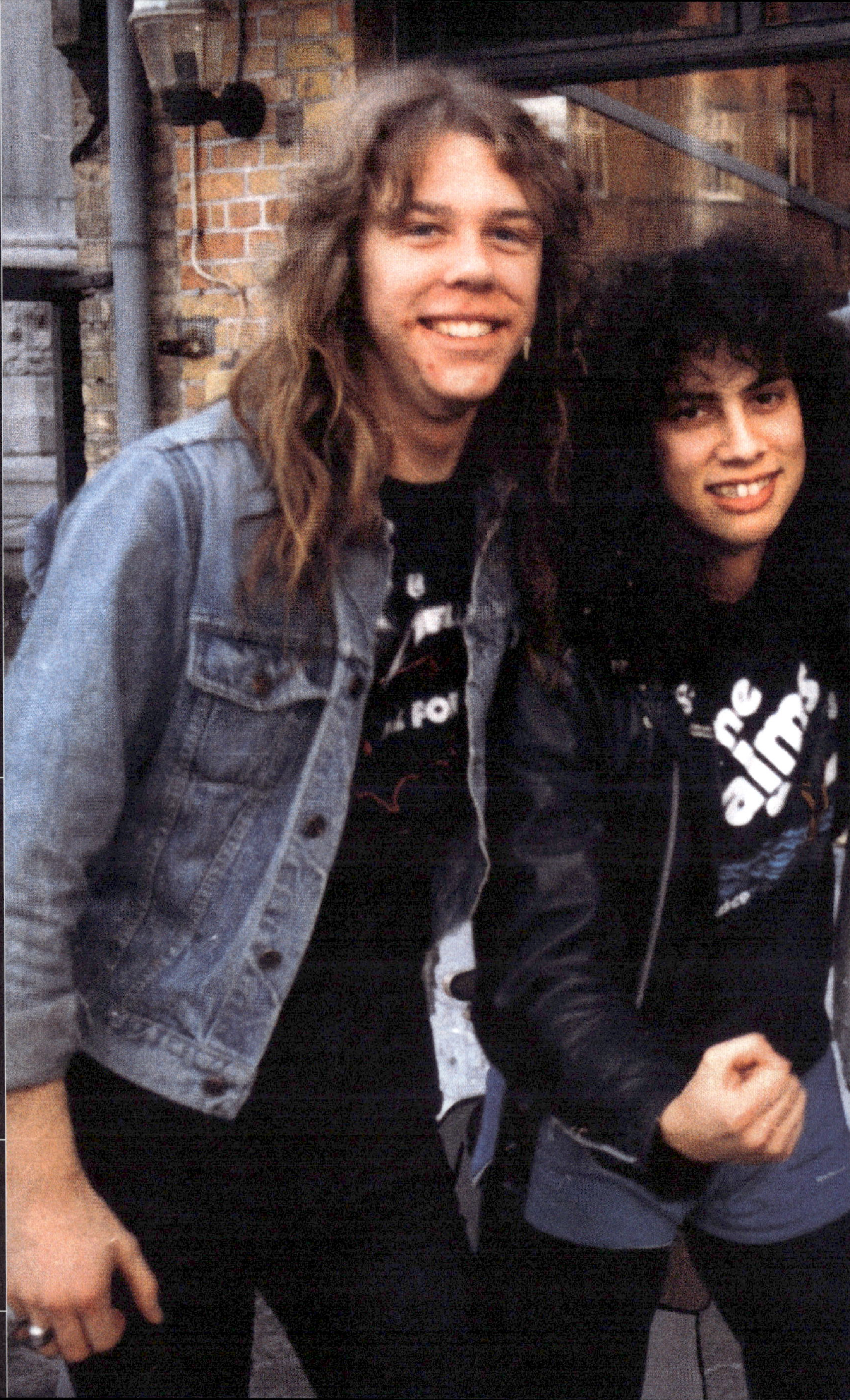

Metallica

Maeke-Blyde - Poperinge

12-02-1984

rumpsteak-salade 220
...ak au poivre 280
steak au champignon 290
...ak provençale
...honade-salade
...de bœuf-mar...

SUPRA

Forty years back on a Sunday, Venom's 'Seven Dates of Hell' tour hit up Poperinge. The crowd was pumped for Venom, but Metallica, the opener, wasn't exactly on everyone's radar yet. The venue wasn't packed, just a handful of fans rushed up front for Metallica's set. But man, after three or four songs, the band had the whole joint in their pocket. A legendary show! *Frederick Moulaert, photographer*

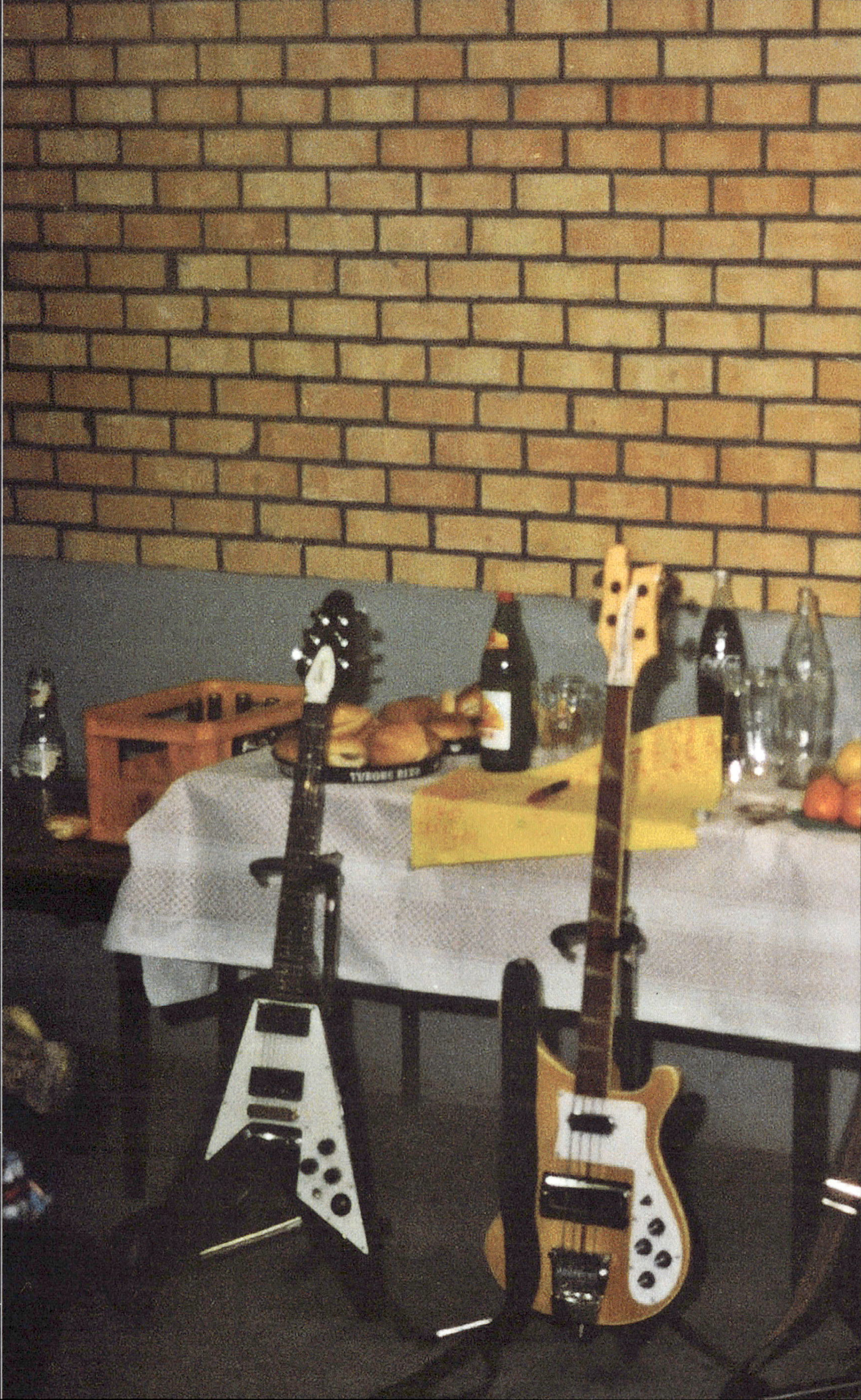

I went for a pee, minding my own business, when I heard this weird noise. Like, heavy thunder mixed with some low-frequency vibes. I didn't even bother to finish up—I sprinted back into the hall. Turns out, it was Cliff Burton shredding a bass solo. Imagine grooving to a bass solo with a damp spot on my pants... Ah, those were the days! *Patrick Goethals*

They were cool blokes. I remember Lars Ulrich asking about the shirt I had on. Ended up swapping it for a Metal Up Your Ass tee. We hit it off, had a blast on the tour, proper laughs all around.

At the final gig in Belgium, we played a prank on Lars—we chopped his drumsticks in half and dusted his snare drum with talcum powder. Then, we rigged firework under his drum stage. When he started drumming, his sticks snapped, talcum powder went flying, and he nearly choked while the drums went kaboom underneath him. Classic! And to top it off, we lobbed rotten tomatoes at them, like, 'Welcome to the club, you've been Venomised!' They took it all in their stride, even though we messed with their set big time. *Conrad 'Cronos' Lant, Venom*

The Venom tour was our first Euro trip. We decided to jump in and let me tell you, it blew our minds! But it put us in the right direction. Lars, having Danish roots, was the only one of us who had already clocked up some serious miles around the globe. *Kirk Hammett, Metallica*

So, my mentor was a real jazz cat. One day, he pulled me aside and goes, "What's up with these dudes? They can't even play." And I'm like, "Who cares, man? Just feel that energy!" *Flemming Rasmussen, Sweet Silence Studio in Denmark during the recording of 'Ride the Lightning' in 1984*

So, I'm thinking I'm all worldly after a few months in NYC. But Europe was a completely different story. James, Cliff, and me? We were in for a shocker. Food, language, shops opening whenever they feel like it, Sundays feeling like ghost towns—all of it. And don't even get me started on the TV—a total mind-boggler, we couldn't understand a word. It took us a while to find our feet. It wasn't what we were expecting, that's for sure. *Kirk Hammett, Metallica*

Before the release of 'At War With Satan', Metallica supported Venom on their 'Seven Dates of Hell' tour. This was the first time the young American band had been introduced to European audiences. But they didn't hang around at the bottom of the ladder for long. Soon enough, they were ruling the roost, leaving their old heroes in the dust. If Venom had recognised the potential of thrash metal back in 1984, they could have hitched a ride on that rocket. *Metal Review*

Metallica pushed the boundaries of the underground metal movement considerably. I think I speak for all truly dedicated metal fans when I wish Lars Ulrich, James Hetfield, Kirk Hammett and Cliff Burton world domination. *Metal Forces, 1984*

Rewind six months. Picture me cruising over the Bay Bridge in my Volkswagen, vodka in hand, blasting Venom at full volume. Headed to some metal gig downtown San Francisco. Next, we were out on tour with them. That was a giant leap for me. I went from hardcore metalhead in the crowd to actually being on stage, as part of the scene. *Kirk Hammett, Metallica, in Rolling Stone*

Talk about the sensation of the century! These four American heavyweights hit us hard with their insane, lightning-fast tunes. On stage, they were simply awesome. The sound system took a hit for the first four songs, but the rest of their set sounded great. *From Tytan fanzine, the Netherlands*

© Rudy De Doncker

✝✝✝✝✝✝✝✝✝✝✝✝✝

I'm convinced: kids who like Priest, Maiden,
KISS and Twisted Sister will pick us up. It won't
happen overnight, but gradually. Metallica could be
at the forefront of a new movement in heavy metal.

Kirk Hammett, Metallica

✝✝✝✝✝✝✝✝✝✝✝✝✝

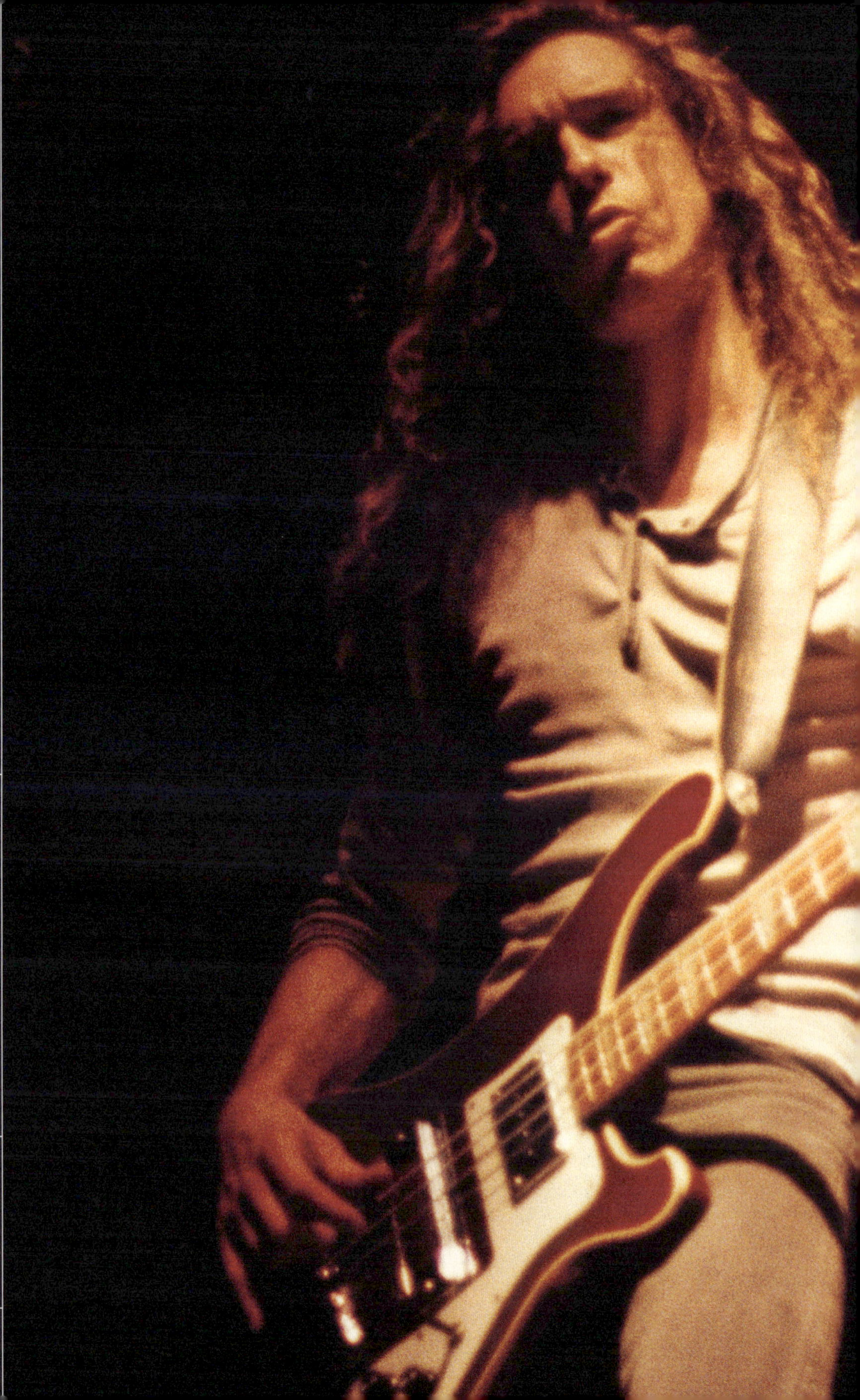

Double impact: Metallica at Heavy Sound '84

Back in '84, Metallica rolled into Poperinge not once, not twice, but three times. After their debut gig at the Maeke-Blyde in February, they hit up the Heavy Sound Festival. Sharing the stage with big names like Lita Ford, Mercyful Fate, and headliners Twisted Sister and Motörhead. Metallica thrashed the field for just 50 minutes. Backstage demands? Two crates of Carlsberg, 25 sandwiches, a cake, and 3 kilos of fresh fruit.

Mathias Danneels, broadcaster and journalist, recalls: "I was covering the 'Betonmolen' column for the teen mag *Joepie*, which was sponsoring the fest. Before that, the record company had flown me out to Copenhagen to catch the band in the studio. Afterwards, I wrote: 'Uriah Heep, Black Sabbath, Deep Purple, move over. There's something totally new in town, and it's called Metallica.' Bagging the first big article about Metallica in Flemish press got me some sort of VIP access. I spent hours at the bar with the lads in Poperinge. Lars Ulrich was the band's main man at the time. Cliff Burton was around too, but seemed to be in a world of his own."

Festival organiser Rik Stael reminisces: "It was a wild festival. We even got the 'most pints per punter' award from Stella Artois: 12! You don't see that kind of boozefest at one-day festivals these days. Thanks to those 8,000 thirsty punters, we covered our costs alright. Bands were still affordable back then, but just the Stageco stage alone set us back 750,000 Belgian francs (about 18,600 euros). Slayer cost us $2,000, Metallica a fair bit less. In '85, a biker gang was accused of grave-robbing after the Slayer gig. I still think politics played a part in that one."

RIDER METALLICA

Artists:
2 cases carlsberg
6 b. mineral water 1/1
4 b. orange juice
1 l. milk

25 assorted sandwiches
   (salads/cheese/meat)
1 cake
3 kg fruit
coffee and tea available
   throughout the day

5 hot meals

50 cups
12 towels

5 artists back stage   } ok
1 ticket artists parking

Crew:
1 case coca-cola
6 b. orange juice

25 assorted sandwiches
   (salads/cheese/meat)
1 cake

8 hot meals

50 cups

8 crew back stage   } ok
2 tickets artists parking

+ 5 T Shirts

Metallica

Heavy Sound Festival '84 - Poperinge

10-06-1984

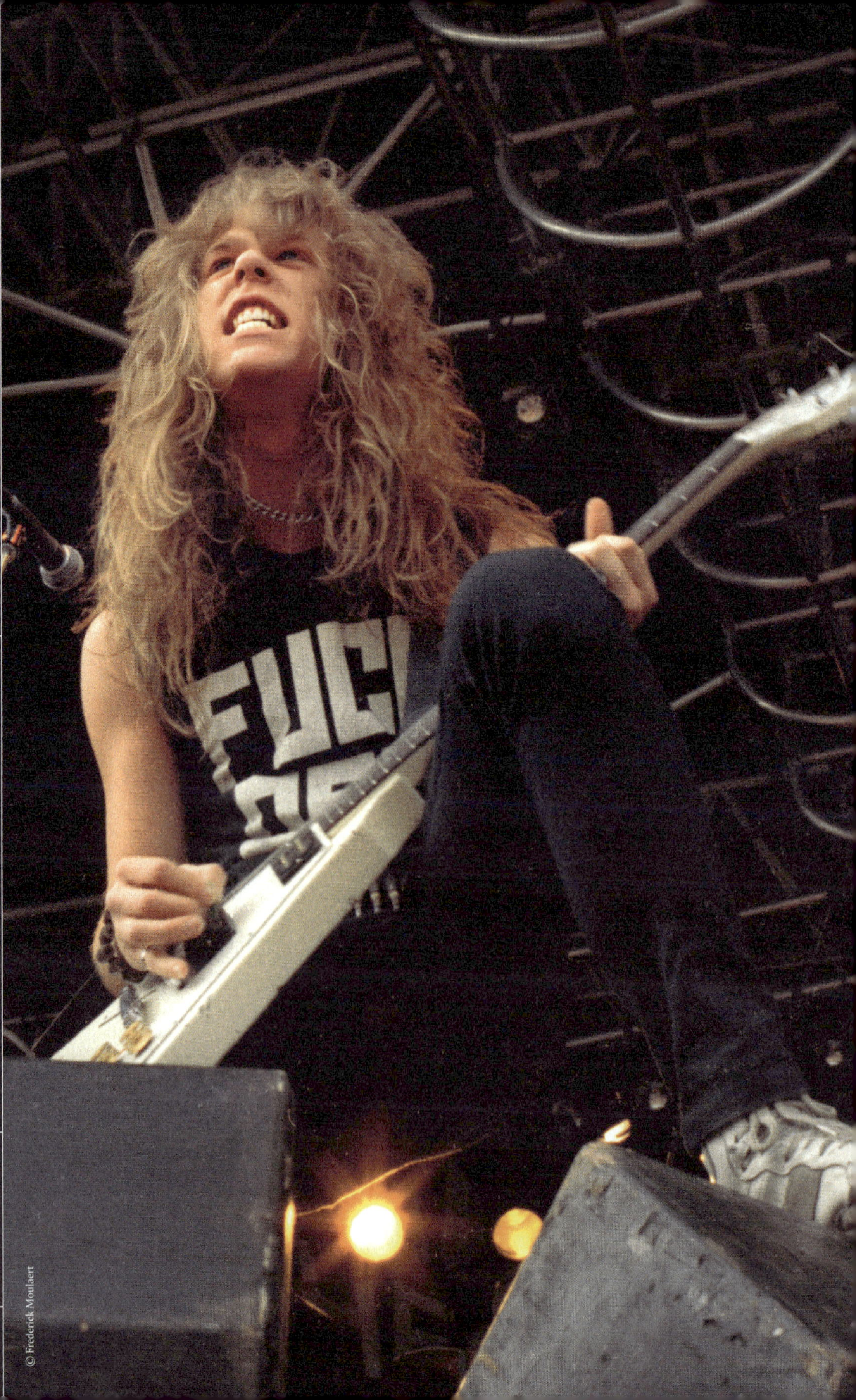

© Frederick Moulaert

Metallica

© Rudy De Doncker

✝✝✝✝✝✝✝✝✝✝✝✝

Uriah Heep,
Black Sabbath,
Deep Purple, move over.
We have heard something
completely new,
and it's called Metallica.

Mathias Danneels

✝✝✝✝✝✝✝✝✝✝✝✝✝

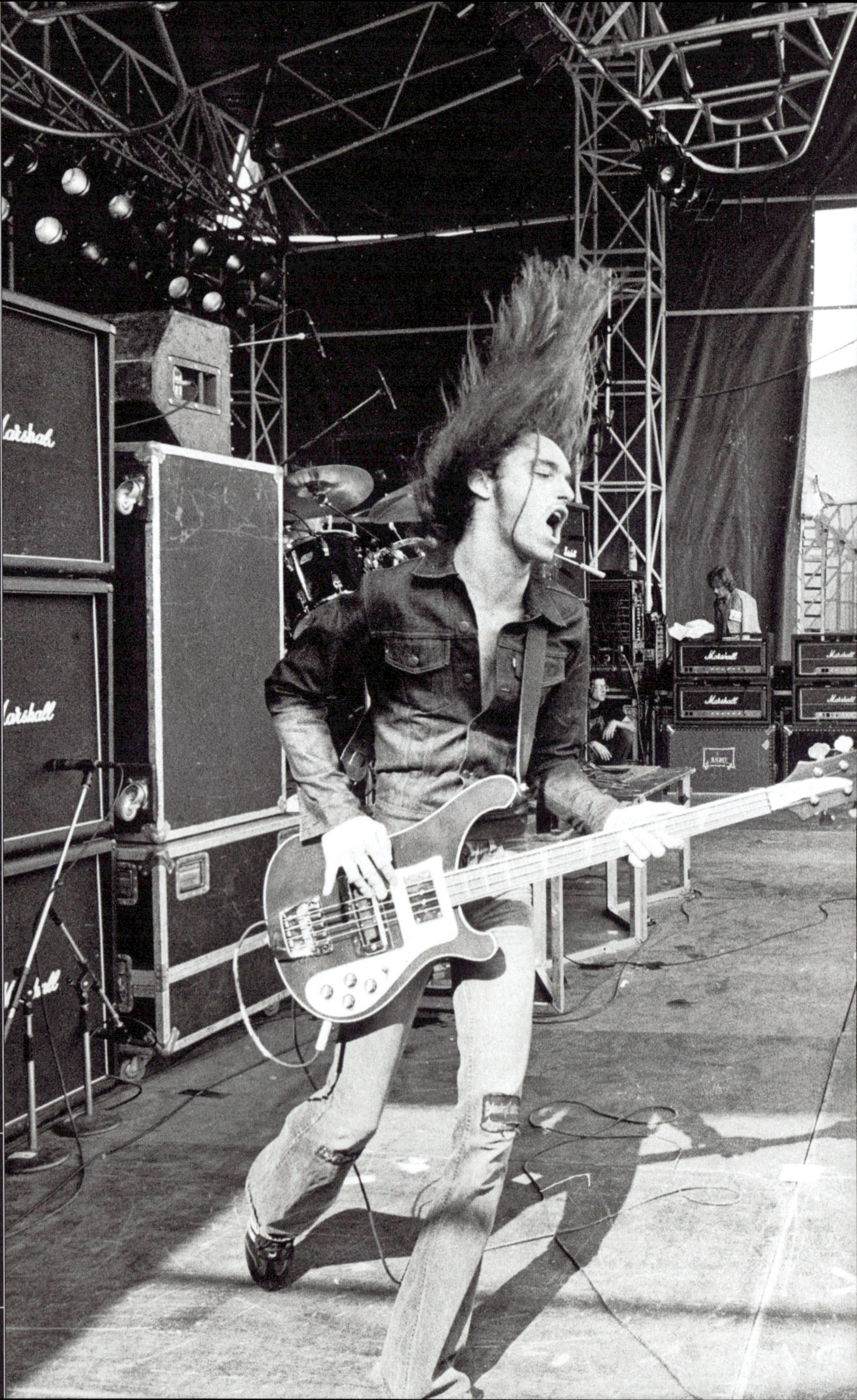
Marshall

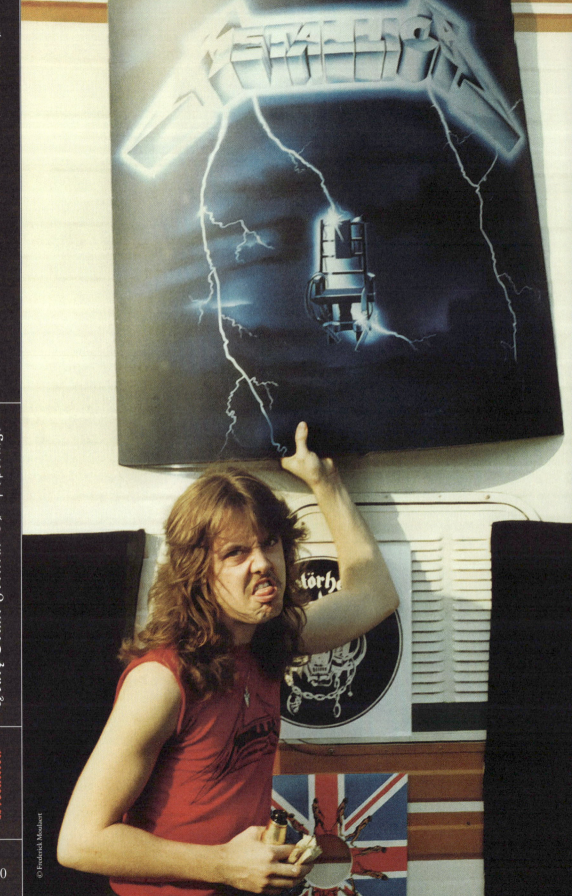

© Frederick Moulaert

© PG Brunelli

PODIUM

Heavy Sound Festival '84 - Poperinge

Metallica

284

© PG Brunelli

Metallica

↓↓↓↓↓↓↓↓↓↓↓↓↓

Cliff Burton was a classically trained musician. Some people reckon he's the ultimate metal bassist. He'd rip it up on his bass like he was shredding on a lead guitar. His one-of-a-kind style shaped Metallica's iconic sound back in the '80s. And then, he was taken from us in a tragic accident on Metallica's tour bus when he was just 24, which adds to his legendary status.

↓↓↓↓↓↓↓↓↓↓↓↓↓

Third time's the charm

On Metallica's third swing by Poperinge in '84, they were on their first-ever European tour as headliner. The support act was Tank. Turns out they were one of James Hetfield's favourite bands. Unfortunately, their set didn't quite hit the mark. It was like a noise explosion, with songs blending into one another and Algy Ward's vocals sounding rough as nails. Meanwhile, the crowd was getting really warmed up, flexing their neck muscles. Tank wrapped it up in just 20 minutes, making way for the boys from San Francisco.

Maeke-Blyde was jam-packed with around 2,000 die-hard Metallica fans. Thirty minutes later, the lights dimmed, the Metallica logo lit up, and the speakers started humming. Then, the acoustic intro to 'Fight Fire With Fire' kicked in. The place exploded, especially when that opening riff hit. I was near the speakers and almost got knocked against the wall!

Metallica kept the fire burning with 'Phantom Lord' and 'The Four Horsemen'. Cliff Burton stole the show with his legendary bass solo 'Pulling Teeth'. 'For Whom the Bell Tolls' kept the vibe going, before cranking up the speed with 'Trapped Under Ice'. A guitar glitch from Kirk Hammett led to 'Call of Ktulu' with James handling the intro solo on his own.

So, once they sorted out the technical hiccup, it was time for some of Metallica's heaviest hitters. The crowd went nuts during 'No Remorse'. 'Seek and Destroy' got so intense, a few kids had to be carried out. And for 'Whiplash', only the most hardcore metalheads were left standing. It was a madhouse!

Metallica gave it their all, dripping sweat as they ripped up the stage. As encores, they busted out their new single 'Creeping Death' with Kirk treating us to a killer guitar solo, building up to an epic climax. And because the crowd was so ecstatic they threw in a blistering version of Diamond Head's 'Am I Evil?' for good measure. But they weren't done yet. The band came back for one last blast, with a medley of 'Jump in the Fire' and 'Motorbreath'. The organisers finally called it a night, and the lights came back on. It was way past midnight, but man, what a legendary gig! *Concert review by Metal Mania*

Maeke-Blyde - Poperinge

Metallica

Discover the making-of video of this photo shoot in Maeke-Blyde, Poperinge on 17 November 1984.

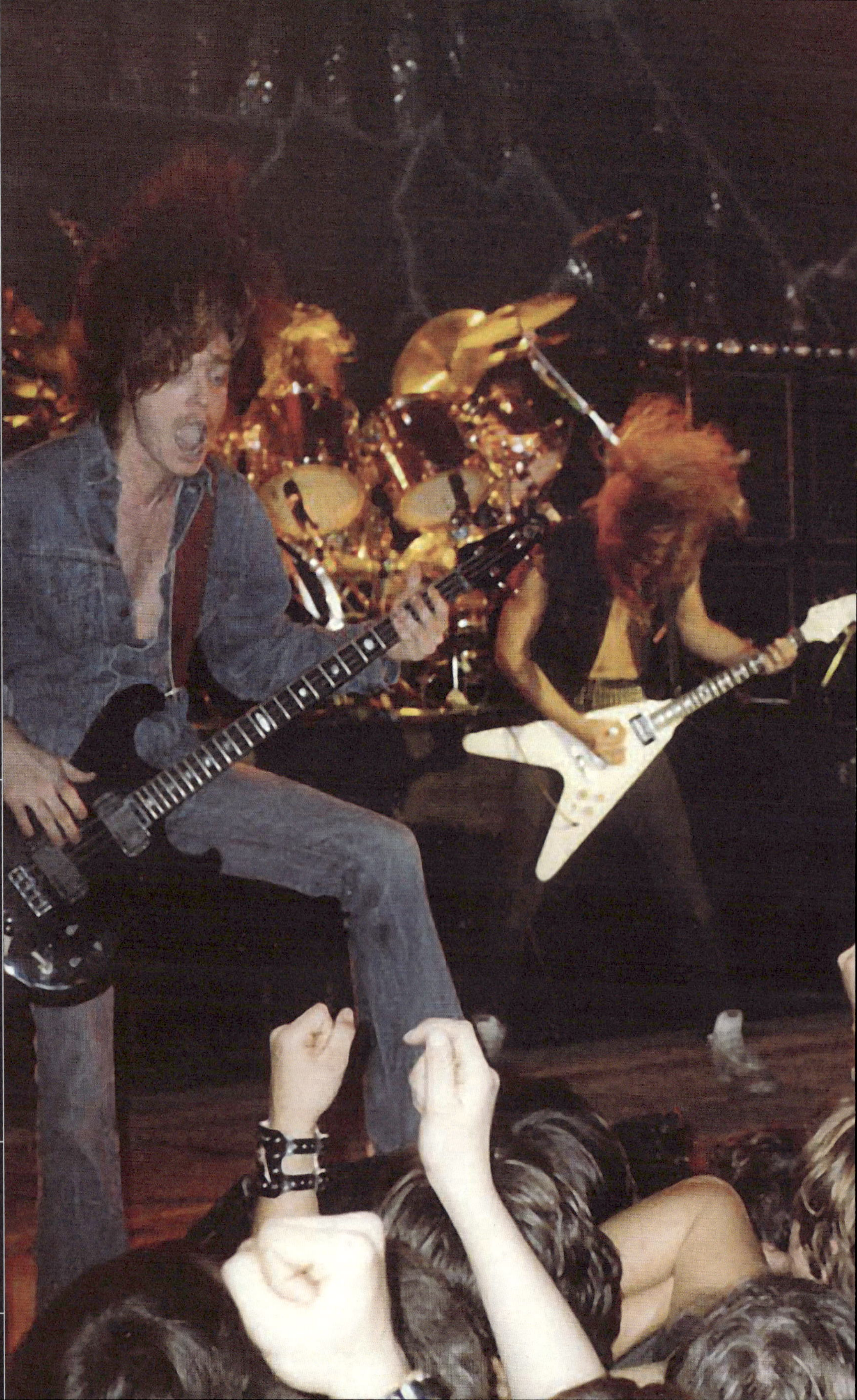

17-11-1984

Maeke-Blyde - Poperinge

Those shows in Poperinge will be etched in my memory forever. Especially the November gig at Maeke-Blyde—utter madness! Metallica went from opening act to headliner in less than a year. The place was packed, tickets sold out like hotcakes. The band were like dervishes of energy, they played so loud it almost blew my ears off.

I caught Metallica three times in Poperinge. First time was in the same venue, and even then, they blew Venom off the stage. 'Kill 'Em All' had just dropped, it was pure brutality. Back then, metal was mainly about love songs, spandex, and flowing locks. Thank goodness things have changed for the better! I'm still a die-hard Metallica fan, and that's not going to change, not even when I'm six feet under. *Ronny Baert*

Back in the day, I was nuts about Tank. I'd go and see all of their gigs at the old Marquee Club in London, even recording almost every show. Then one day, out of the blue, Algy, the singer/bassplayer of the band, comes up to me and goes, 'Hey, why don't you join the band?' Next thing I know, I'm touring Europe with them. It was unreal, mate. We dove straight into working on the 'Honour and Blood' album, and before I knew it, we were tagging along with Metallica on their 'Ride the Lightning' tour in '84—the year they hit it big. I still remember the first time I saw those guys, soundchecking for the first show. It was like nothing I'd heard before, they were amazing. It was the third time they played that same venue that year, and the place was packed to the brim. Pure magic. *Cliff 'the riff' Evans, Tank*

It's the summer of '84, and hard rock is in a comfortable position. MTV's blowing up, and you've got the likes of hairbands Bon Jovi and Ratt claiming the airwaves and charts. But then, from the foggy streets of San Francisco, comes Metallica. Through the mist and the madness, their second album, 'Ride the Lightning', hits like a bolt from the blue. Suddenly, that commercial hard rock vibe starts to fade into the background. Metallica were on a totally different level. They hit the road like there's no tomorrow, touring non-stop. And no band had ever done three shows in one year on European soil, let alone in Belgium! But Metallica understood from day one that Europe had a vibrant metal scene. European headbangers were hungry for speed and thrash metal, and were way ahead of the game compared to the US crowds.

Tank, one of James Hetfield's favourite bands, opened for Metallica on their third gig in Poperinge.

‡‡‡‡‡‡‡‡‡‡‡‡‡

Metallica was already blowing minds with 'Kill 'Em All'. And when 'Ride the Lightning' came out, the hype was off the charts. Their sound was a total game-changer. And that gig in Poperinge? Insane! They unleashed this unseen combo of speed, aggression, and precision. And this show was the first time ever they played 'Trapped Under Ice'. Picture James Hetfield, just 20 years old with a face full of pimples, chilling with fans on the grass outside. Those laidback vibes were what made Heavy Sound gigs so special. *Geert Ryssen*

‡‡‡‡‡‡‡‡‡‡‡‡‡

Three weeks before Metallica's third gig, we were going all out with our promo campaign. I'm out there, putting up posters in Kortrijk where I probably shouldn't have been. And so I got busted by the police. They haul me off, in my own car no less, to the police station. Spent the whole night in a cell.

Next morning, I'm face to face with the big chief, a real fatherly type. They gave me back my car, but my posters and glue? Confiscated. And even worse: ALL my posters were in that car. So, three weeks before the gig, I'm left high and dry without any posters. Ended up scrambling to get a new batch made in record time from Steen Screenprinters. *Jean-Pierre Staelen*

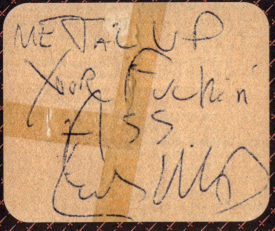

METAL UP
YOUR Fuckin'
ASS
[signature]

NO LIFE 'TIL
VODKA!
[signature]

GREAT
FUCKIN'
PICTURE!
[signatures]

21/4 - 7/6   650 Fr.   Zo 10 juni 1984 om 11u.00   deuren open
               35 gulden   Bosco Sportterreinen - Poperinge (B)   om 9u.00
               100 FF   Di 10 Juin 1984 à 11h.00   portes ouvertes
               35 DM   Bosco Terrain pour sports, Poperinge (B)   à 9h.00
HEAVY   Sun 10th June 1984 at 11 a.m.   doors open
SOUND FESTIVAL 84   Bosco Sportfields - Poperinge (B)   at 9 a.m.
№ 09626   750 Fr.   All glass, cans, firecrackers, iron objects
               40 gulden   and other dangerous things are strictly
10/6   120 FF   prohibited on the festival-area. This is for
               40 DM   your own safety and for the safety of other
                                people. No camera's and recorders allowed.
                                Everyone will be searched. God bless you

(Not valuable without the tear-off-slip)

[signature]

21/4 - 7/6   650 Fr.   Zo 10 juni 1984 om 11u.00   deuren open
               35 gulden   Bosco Sportterreinen - Poperinge (B)   om 9u.30
               100 FF   Di 10 Juin 1984 à 11h.00   portes ouvertes
               35 DM   Bosco Terrain pour sports, Poperinge (B)   à 9h.00
HEAVY   Sun 10th June 1984 at 11 a.m.   doors open
SOUND FESTIVAL 84   Bosco Sportfields - Poperinge (B)   at 9 a.m.
№ 12966   750 Fr.   All glass, cans, firecrackers, iron objects
               40 gulden   and other dangerous things are strictly
10/6   120 FF   prohibited on the festival-area. This is for
               40 DM   your own safety and for the safety of other
                                people. No camera's and recorders allowed.
                                Everyone will be searched. God bless you

(Not valuable without the tear-off-slip)

FOR PATRICK

[signature]

VODKA
+
COKE
THE BON

MUSIC MAN   **music man**
              record shops   **JOEPIE**
                                         BETONMOLEN
Brugge: Niklaas Desparstraat 1
Gent: Bagattenstraat 197
                                         IF IT AIN'T HEAVY
J-CARD CONNECTION   **IT AIN'T ON**
                                         MAUSOLEUM
BaC **PERSOONLIJKE**
         BANKSERVICE

KILL '
[signature]

LARS ULRICH
(METALLICA)

POPERINGE (B)

ZAAL MAECKE-BLYDE

DIMANCHE ZONDAG	12	FEVRIER FEBRUARI	1984	A TE	20	H u

IN CONCERT

TICKETS & INFO : 051/20 12 00

AALST : Solbemol
BRUGGE : Bilbo, Music Man, Flemish Record Store
BRUSSEL : Caroline Music
DIKSMUIDE : De locomotief
GENT : Bilbo, Music Man

GENK : Cinderella
HASSELT : Hittip
IEPER : Happy Days
IZEGEM : Elpee Shop
KORTRIJK : Popcenter, Ad Fundum
LICHTERVELDE : 't Schild
MENEN : De Krimson
NIEUWPOORT : Disco-bar

OOSTENDE : Popcenter
POPERINGE : Keikop, Ons Huis, Hoppebel, Delbaere
ROESELARE : Ad Fundum, Billboard, Piet Gein
TORHOUT : Bufallo, Haiko Club
TOURNAI : Tournai Disques
VEURNE : De Corner
WAREGEM : De Klub
WERVIK : Les Copains

ARMENTIERES : Studio Panez
DUNKERQUE : Et. Rouvroy
LILLE : Fnac, Popson

HARDROCK - CAFE
AD FUNDUM
KORTRIJK - ROESELARE

PoPCENTER
KORTRIJK - OOSTENDE

V.U./ VAN ZEGEL   Verantw. uitg.: Afzender zie: Mrtsenlaat 19. Roeselare (B)

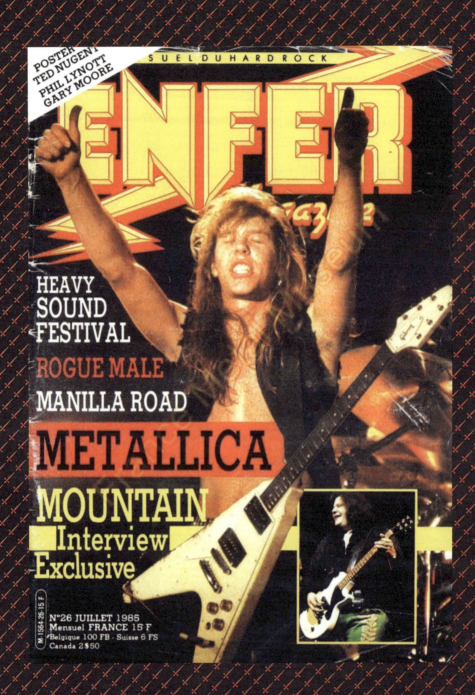

In CONCERT

METALLICA

POPERINGE (B) ~ MAECKEBLYDE
Saturday 17 November '84 20u.

* Support act

VU v.z.w ABASTIE concerts 051 20 12 00

KULTUREEL DOEL ART.19B

TICKETS
AALST: Solbemol
ANTWERPEN. Brabo
BRUGGE Bilbo
BRUGGE Music Man
GENT: Bilbo
GENT: Music Man
KORTRIJK: Popcenter
ROESELARE Billboard
tickets 350-380fr. 55-60ff.
zeefdruk steen 050/21 22 80

POPERINGE Ons Huis.
Keikop.
Deibaere
Hoppeber
TORHOUT Hako Club
IZEGEM: Elpee Shop
BRUSSEL : Caroline
WERVIK: Pomper
IEPER: Happy Days

OOSTENDE : Popcenter
WAREGEM. Klup
MENEN. De Krimson
KORTRIJK, Ad Fundum
DIKSMUIDE Music express
LILLE (F), Fnac. Papson
DUNKERQUE. Et Rourty
TOURNAI : Tournai Disques

POPCENTER
KORTRIJK - OOSTENDE
056 21 94 89   059 80 38 53

ASLK
we doen met je mee

RIDE THE LIGHTNING
METALLICA
with special guests:
TANK

POPERINGE (B)   Maecke-Blijde - 20.00 h.
Saturday 17 november '84

IN CONCERT

METALLICA

+ SUPPORT ACT

№ 0355

TICKETS : 350 - 380 BFR
55 - 60 FF

Druk Verduyn pvba - 8810 Rumbeke

METALLICA
TANK

POPERINGE   17-11-84

NAME :

FUNCTION:
BACK-STAGE

METALLICA
TANK

POPERINGE   17-11-84

NAME : FILTHY EDDY

FUNCTION: GUEST V.I.P.
BACK-STAGE

METALLICA
TANK

POPERINGE   17-11-84

NAME :

FUNCTION:

DIMANCHE 26 MAI '85 - 11h
POPERINGE - BELGIQUE

HEAVY SOUND FESTIVAL 3

BASF
MUSIC GETS ITS 3RD DIMENSION

WARLOCK ~ CROSSFIRE
TOBRUK ~ TOKYO BLADE
PRETTY MAIDS
LEE AARON
SLAYER SPECIAL GUEST
UFO NEW LINE UP

JOEPIE BETONMOLEN

INFO : HEAVY SOUND. Luc WAEYAERT, Populiereweg 79 - 8280 KOEKELARE
19-32-51/58.08.48 (Festivalphone 19-32-57/33.71.83)
Avec l'autocar au HEAVY SOUND FESTIVAL (festivalphone : (057) 33 71 83)

LILLE Association Rock Contacts 14, Rue de Bergues
59000 LILLE   Frederick BEPIRZEZ   (016) 87 51 54
LIEGE - Alain Sarlet - Rue de Harlez 5, LIEGE
TOURNAI - Jean-Marc MONTEGNIES, Rue des marteaux 2, LESDAIN

(020) 53 35 47
(020) 86 26 55
(041) 53 17 11
(069) 34 51 64

MUSIC MAN
RECORD SHOPS
BRUGGE GENT

Stella Artois

BASF
MUSIC GETS ITS 3RD DIMENSION

✝✝✝✝✝✝

Heavy Sound Festival 1985

Every year, Heavy Sound was upping its game. The organisers were getting more professional, the budget was getting bigger, and even the posters were getting an upgrade. 1985 was set to be the ultimate edition. But just after the festival wrapped up, things took a wild turn. Some fools went and messed with a grave in a nearby cemetery, sparking off a whole political saga.

More hard rock, less metal
Right after the 1984 edition, they gave the green light for Heavy Sound 1985. The council and the police were happy with how things went down. And after the first gig in Poperinge, people weren't as jumpy anymore. Restaurant and shop owners were loving it—festival-goers were spending their cash left and right. But this year, things were going to be somewhat different. The organisers decided to dial it back a bit, and tone down the headbanging vibes. Less metal, more hard rock—kind of like putting the concrete mixer on a lower gear.

Towards a monoculture
When the Heavy Sound crew decided to switch gears towards more hard rock, finding a headline act got real tricky. The big names in hard rock often had huge agencies backing them up, making negotiations a pain in the ass. Plus, these bands didn't quite have the punk attitude of their speed and thrash metal counterparts.

Organiser Luc Waeyaert had been talking to Deep Purple for ages, but then some big-shot Belgian booker swooped in and shut it down. Next up, Judas Priest and Ozzy Osbourne were eyeing a spot on the lineup. The organisers even thought about changing the festival date to fit their tight tour schedules. But when these agencies slapped on exorbitant price tags, Heavy Sound had to bail out.

It was like the start of a whole new era. As the music business was getting all pro, only the big bookers could pay for the top acts.

In the end, the freshly reunited UFO got the headline spot. They had tons of classics up their sleeve, but it was a bit of a departure from the heavy-hitting lineup of '84. To keep the hardcore fans happy, the organisers managed to rope in the hottest thrash band around:

Slayer. It was their only show in continental Europe that year, and damn, did they tear the place apart! By then, they were starting to wear out their welcome in a lot of venues with their excessive fireworks and smoke bombs.

Germans, outlaws and a phone box
The festival once again landed the Don Bosco sports ground. But this time, they're taking over the bigger field where they usually do pony races in the summer. How's that for change of scenery? This field was used to getting trampled underhoof, but now it was about to get bulldozed by metalheads from all over. Once again there was weekend camping, this time for a small fee. No less than a quarter of the visitors came from abroad.

During the '84 edition, German fans wreaked some havoc. So, the organisers doubled up on security this time, pumping up the budget to 400,000 Belgian francs. The night before the festival, the vibe was surprisingly chill. The restaurants in Poperinge were all about hospitality, pulling overtime shifts. And metalheads were working that overtime too, but on the other side of the bar. In the end, the only bit of trouble was three young hoodlums wrecking a phone box in the market square. The security - this time, the infamous Outlaws biker gang - sorted the culprits out and turned them over to the police. But guess who had to pay the bill? Yep, you got it—the Heavy Sound crew. That was a first setback.

Musically rock-solid
Sunday's lineup kicked off with the powerhouse Warlock from Germany, hitting the stage at 11 in the morning. Frontwoman Doro Pesch had everyone who was awake absolutely hooked. And for the first time, the sound was spot-on—the professionalism paid off.

Next up was Belgian pride Crossfire, who came prepared with their own festival posters. They brought some real heavy vibes and picked up the pace. Then came Tobruk, steering us back into hard rock territory. Apparently, they were part of a package deal with UFO, and the crowd wasn't entirely sold. Pretty Maids from Scandinavia warmed things up nicely, even though some fanzine journos were a bit bummed about a synthesizer creeping into their set.

Tokyo Blade hit the stage next, wrestling with some tech issues, but frontman Vic Wright kept the energy going strong. Canadian Lee Aaron made us all break a sweat, not just from headbanging. The Metal Queen herself had the whole crowd eating out of the palm of her hand.

But let's get real—when Slayer unleashed their fury, it was like the whole festival came alive. As a metal storm of evil guitar riffs blasted across the field, the grass was almost set ablaze. Slayer blew everyone away, sounding even faster and harder than on their records.

After that intense ride, UFO's melodic hard rock was a bit of a shift, but those seasoned rockers knew how to keep the crowd going. They had to come back for an encore, proving they were the perfect closing act.

The festival made the headlines like never before, even though the crowd size stayed the same—around 8,000 metalheads. Heavy Sound was officially on the map in the festival world. And on

✝✝✝✝✝✝✝✝✝✝✝✝✝

When Slayer unleashed their fury, it was like the whole festival came alive. As a metal storm of evil guitar riffs blasted across the field, the grass was almost set ablaze. Slayer blew everyone away, sounding even faster and harder than on their records.

✝✝✝✝✝✝✝✝✝✝✝✝✝

Monday, the Poperinge town council was stoked about how smoothly everything went down.

But still, skirmishes on Friday and Saturday were a real downer for the organisers. Last year, they sorted out all the compensation claims, but this time, there was some serious abuse. Some claims were completely made up. And it turns out, some of the leftover booze went missing during the cleanup. So they most likely weren't festival-goers. It's the classic tale of a passion project getting out of hand. So, by Monday, the organisers were already talking about calling it quits. Enough was enough.

The untimely passing
Things got worse on Tuesday when they found out someone had dug up a grave. Turns out, some so-called 'fans' took this whole satanism thing a bit too seriously. And then, a few local politicians decided to add insult to injury.

Henri d'Udekem d'Akoz, leader of the opposition, wasted no time blowing up the whole mess and pointing fingers at the town council. Turns out he went and made snapshots of the desecrated grave himself, saying he wanted to make sure nothing got swept under the rug. But then, a cemetery worker spilled the beans, saying he only opened the grave because d'Udekem d'Akoz insisted. Then, things got even flakier when d'Udekem d'Akoz got charged for messing with the grave. His response? He slammed back with a lawsuit for defamation. It was like a political circus, and the whole thing just got too much for the organisation to handle. So they decided to throw in the towel, there and then.

Heavy Sound went from a small-time metal gig to a full-blown fest in just three years. Those lineup names still give people who love hard rock and metal goosebumps. The organisers were totally plugged into the metal scene. That final nail in the coffin wasn't fair. But looking back, it was the festival's vibe that really sealed its fate. Heavy Sound just didn't belong in that ultra-pro world with big-shot agencies and piles of paperwork. For them, it was all about the music, not the money. And that's how it should be. But alas, all things must pass.

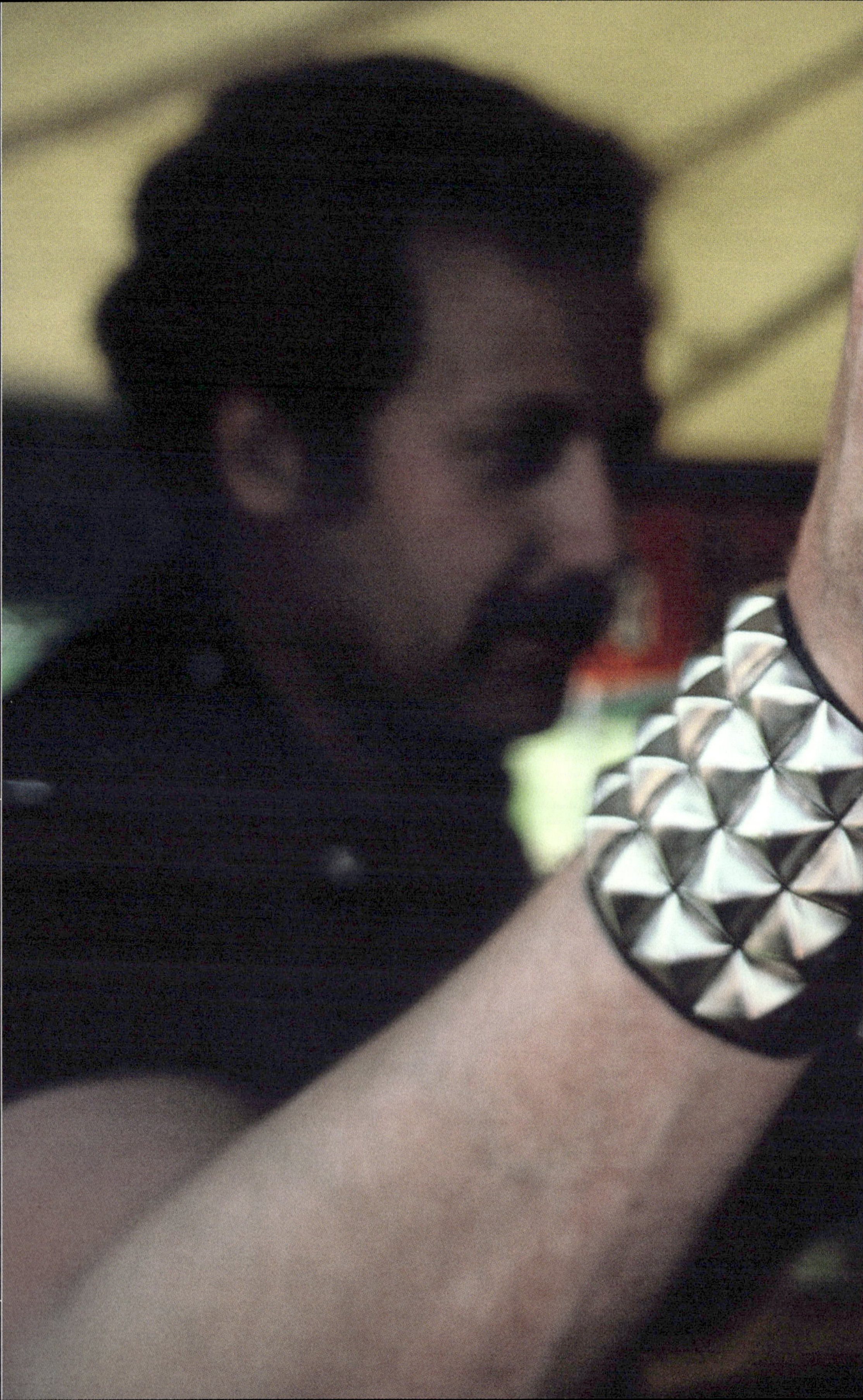

Heavy Sound Festival '85 - Poperinge

26-05-1985

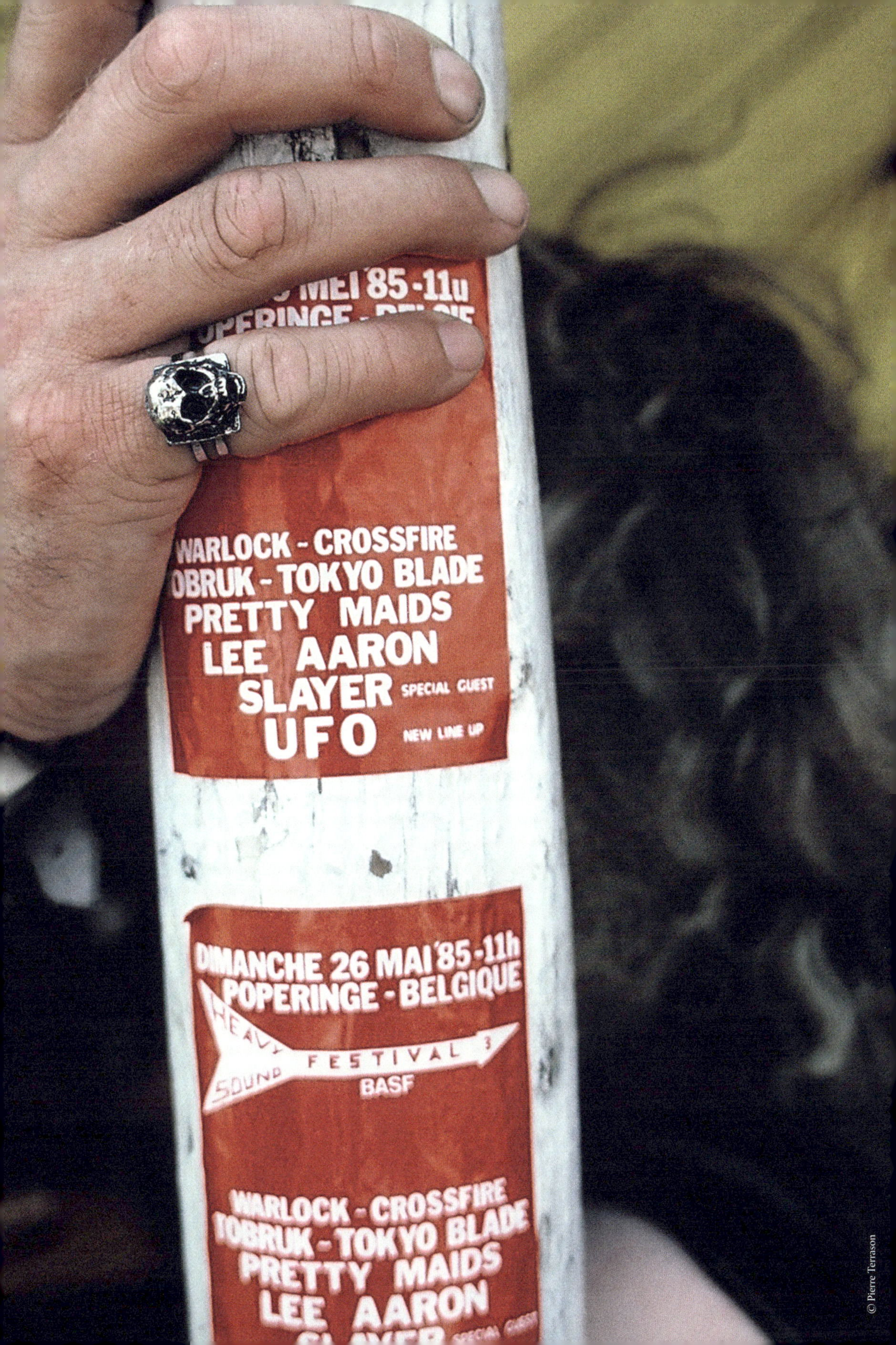

WARLOCK - CROSSFIRE
OBRUK - TOKYO BLADE
PRETTY MAIDS
LEE AARON
SLAYER SPECIAL GUEST
UFO NEW LINE UP

MEI '85 -11u
POPERINGE - BELGIE

DIMANCHE 26 MAI '85 -11h
POPERINGE - BELGIQUE

HEAVY
SOUND FESTIVAL 3
BASF

WARLOCK - CROSSFIRE
TOBRUK - TOKYO BLADE
PRETTY MAIDS
LEE AARON
SLAYER SPECIAL GUEST

© Pierre Terrason

Warlock and Lee Aaron, two bands with some
serious girl power, were a deliberate choice.
Herman Schueremans, the mastermind behind it
all, once told me that a fest is all about sex, drugs,
and rock 'n' roll. He said you got to have enough
women in the lineup. Back in '84, we already
had Lita Ford bringing in the crowds.

Luc Waeyaert. Written by Stefan Carlier, Spin City fanzine

© Rudy De Doncker

Ostrogoth, Crossfire and Killer played at Heavy Sound once. But Acid from West Flanders didn't get the chance. They always blamed us for that, but normally they would get the chance at the fourth edition. It was always my intention to feature Belgian groups. The initial idea was that Crossfire would open the third edition. But Mausoleum Records chipped in 40,000 francs to have Crossfire play after Warlock. *Luc Waeyaert. Written by Stefan Carlier, Spin City fanzine*

Alfie Falckenbach from Mausoleum arranged for our faces to be printed on the tickets. And since we were on tour, they let us sneak in for a soundcheck the night before. We crashed in our van for the night and man, it was freezing. I woke up the next morning with my voice completely gone. The doctor gave me two shots—right in my vocal cords. Somehow, I managed to belt it out like a nightingale that day, but I couldn't speak for the next three weeks. *Peter De Wint, Crossfire*

Heavy Sound Festival '85 - Poperinge

Heavy Sound Festival '85 - Poperinge

Crossfire

© Rudy De Doncker

FRONT STAGE

KLEPTO

Tobruk

© Rudy De Doncker

Heavy Sound Festival '85 – Poperinge

Tokyo Blade & Tobruk

© Rudy De Doncker

Heavy Sound Festival '85 - Poperinge

Tokyo Blade

© Frédéric Monbaert

Rudy De Doncker: never surrender

Mixing photography with music gave me the perfect excuse to hang out with awesome people around the globe, and just have a blast. Back in the late '70s, I was totally hooked on concerts and started toting my camera everywhere. Slowly but surely, I built up my portfolio, snapping shots of local bands left and right. Some of them even ended up in hard rock and metal mags.

Then I got the mighty Van Halen in front of my lens, my first big break. That's when I knew: "This is the life for me!" Things really kicked into high gear in '83. Mausoleum Records picked my pics for their Belgian metal compilation album 'If It's Loud, We're Proud', featuring killer bands like Ostrogoth, Crossfire, and Killer. Next, Killer invited me to join them on a UK tour. Those pics even made it into the Betonmolen section of the teen mag Joepie.

More doors swung open, and a year later, I landed the gig as Heavy Sound's festival photographer. My shots were published in mags like Aard-schok, Rock Tribune, Terrorizer, Rock Hard, Metal Hammer, and Metal Edge. I've been blessed with loads of support from bands, which has landed my pics on countless CD and DVD covers.

Fast forward forty years, and I'm still living it up, snapping pics like there's no tomorrow and checking out shows almost every week.
Rudy De Doncker, music photographer at heart and soul

✝✝✝✝✝✝✝✝✝✝✝✝

Although Tokyo Blade had a lot of tech
troubles, the charisma and sheer enthusiasm
of singer Vic Wright kept the band going.
The audience soon overheated.
Some fans called it an early climax.

✝✝✝✝✝✝✝✝✝✝✝✝

Heavy Sound Festival '85 - Poperinge

Tokyo Blade

© Piet Overstijns

© Piet Overstijns

Heavy Sound Festival '85 - Poperinge

Lee Aaron

© Rudy De Doncker

Heavy Sound Festival '85 - Poperinge

Lee Aaron

✝✝✝✝✝✝✝✝✝✝✝✝✝

Bloody hell, Heavy Sound Fest '85... My buddy Christophe and I were there! That lineup was insane. I'll always remember what Tom said at that very first Slayer show in Europe. 'You never forget your first, right?' And don't get me started on Lee Aaron, still got a major crush on her.

Denis Hill

✝✝✝✝✝✝✝✝✝✝✝✝✝

© Frederik Moulaert

My former brigade chief spilled some juicy details about the past. Apparently, the mayor at the time, Marc Mahieu, didn't fully grasp the situation. They ended up arresting so many people that the local jail got overcrowded. Some metalheads even got stuck in the garage grease pit at the police station with just a cop and his dog keeping watch. When they were let out, some refused to empty their pee buckets. Can you imagine? They got lined up against a wall and had those buckets dumped on them. Meanwhile, the whole village held its breath. Only one shop on Deken de Bo lane stayed open, while the others closed up shop. That shopkeeper must've done some booming business. *Dirk Lefebvre, ex-gendarme*

Heavy Sound Festival '85 - Poperinge

© Rudy De Doncker

Slayer

Back in '84, I got my hands on 'Show No Mercy' and had this gut feeling that Slayer was going to shake up the metal scene. Venom was cool and all, but Slayer just totally clicked with me. So when they popped up on the bill for Heavy Sound '85, I just knew I had to be there, even if it meant scraping my last pennies together. I hitched rides all the way from Munich to Brussels, then to Kortrijk where I met up with some fellow metalheads heading to Poperinge. I remember the festival was crawling with cops. And Slayer totally... slayed. They were aggressive and fast. Live, they really had that raw punk edge. I've seen them live countless times since then. *Michael Sholl*

Heavy Sound '85, a day dedicated to just one thing: catching Slayer! We're chilling by the backstage gate when two guys from Pretty Maids stroll out in their stage outfits, checking out the scene. Next, Tom Araya and Dave Lombardo step out, and suddenly everyone's rushing the gate. Those poor Pretty Maids thought they were the hot ticket and started running. Until they realised the commotion was for the Slayer dudes. They just shrugged it off and walked away, classic!

Tom and Dave were loving the unexpected attention, grinning from ear to ear. Slayer ripped through their set on Black Widow's gear, with the band's Henny Tangelder and Leon Goewie from Vengeance pitching in as roadies. By the time UFO hit the stage, the crowd had kind of dissolved. And let's just say Lee Aaron's tight red pants caused quite the stir. No need for further explanation, right? *Pat Genk*

© Frederick Moubaert

Heavy Sound Festival '85 - Poperinge

Slayer

Slayer

Heavy Sound Festival '85 - Poperinge

Slayer

© Rudy De Doncker

Raining blood over Belgium

I landed in London with Slayer on 25 May, 1985, after leaving LA the previous day. We headed straight for the rental company expecting a tour bus, but all we got is this Sprinter van. And they're cramming our gear in there like Tetris blocks, they even took the cabinets out of their cases just to squeeze more in. But still, there was not enough space.

Kerry was ready to throw in the towel and fly back home, but Jeff's like, "No man, we've come too far to bail now over a van!" So, they gave us this photocopy map with 'X' marks for London and Belgium,

like some kind of treasure hunt. Luckily we had the festival info packet with a map of the surrounding area, we just had to find it from London.

Then they handed me the keys, and guess what? Stick shift. And I'd never driven anything other than automatics in my life! So, Tom would get us going, and I think Dave did too. Once we got to the highway, I could drive.

Eventually, we made it to the ferry. But because we didn't have the visas we needed for France, we had to take the longer ferry to Holland instead of the short one to Calais. Finally, we hit Belgium, heading for Poperinge and the Heavy Sound Festival.

Poperinge awaits

We arrived at the festival while opening band Warlock were on stage. When they finished, due to rumors that Slayer weren't playing, an announcement was made that Slayer would be playing.

The promoter looked pretty anxious when we hadn't arrived yet, but once we showed up, he visibly relaxed. He pointed at the crowd and shouted "8,000 people!". "Yeah, fucking huge", I nodded. When he told me "5,000 of them are here for Slayer", I was like "No way!" Backstage, I dropped the bomb on the band: "Guess what? There's 5,000 people out there waiting just for you guys."

The moment Lee Aaron finished her set, the crowd started chanting "Slayer! Slayer! Slayer!" They practically shooed Lee offstage. She didn't come back for an encore.

Because of the long interlude between sets, we asked if Slayer could start earlier. The promoter was cool with that, as long as we stuck to the timetable. So, Slayer got going as soon as they were ready, and they absolutely killed it for a whole hour, even though they were only slated for 50 minutes.

When Slayer walked out in broad daylight, the place went nuts. It was like something out of a metal dream. Believe me, I still get goosebumps thinking of Slayer stepping out on that stage. I mean: an evil metal band making this sunny place go absolutely crazy. There's a cool video of it on

Doug Goodman (2nd from left), Gus Roan (Roadrunner Records, far right), and friends

© Frederick Moulaert

YouTube. And let me tell you, the grins on the band's faces... When they hit that stage, it was pure victory. And when they stepped off stage, it was like witnessing the happiest metal band on the planet.

It was an unforgettable experience. I mean, we were just California kids who'd never been anywhere. We were basically still living with our parents. Yet here they were, conquering Belgium. *Doug Goodman, tour-manager Slayer*

✝✝✝✝✝✝✝✝✝✝✝✝✝

As much as I loved UFO, to me the real headliners of Heavy Sound '85 were Slayer—hands down. I got my hands on a ticket early and decided to use an old white bedsheet to whip up a banner for my Californian heroes. I did my stinking best to recreate the classic Slayer penta-gram-of-swords logo at the kitchen table, which earned me a few crooked looks from mum and dad. In a gothic font – what else! - I wrote 'HAS NO BOUNDARIES' next to it. Spent hours on that labour of love, only to have it trampled in the madness up front, where I was squished against the barriers with a short English bloke on my shoulders for half the gig. The guy thanked me  afterwards with a cold brew, but since beer wasn't my cuppa tea yet, I secretly passed it on to my pal Dirk. *Chris Dexters*

Slayer fraternises with Marc Mahieu,
the mayor of Poperinge.

This photo is without a doubt the strangest memory of the festival. The empty grounds after Heavy Sound. An accidental double take with the ghost of Jeff Hanneman looming through it. He was only 21 when he first played in Europe in '85, right here on this very field.

Jeff Hanneman, Slayer (31 January 1964 - 2 May 2013)

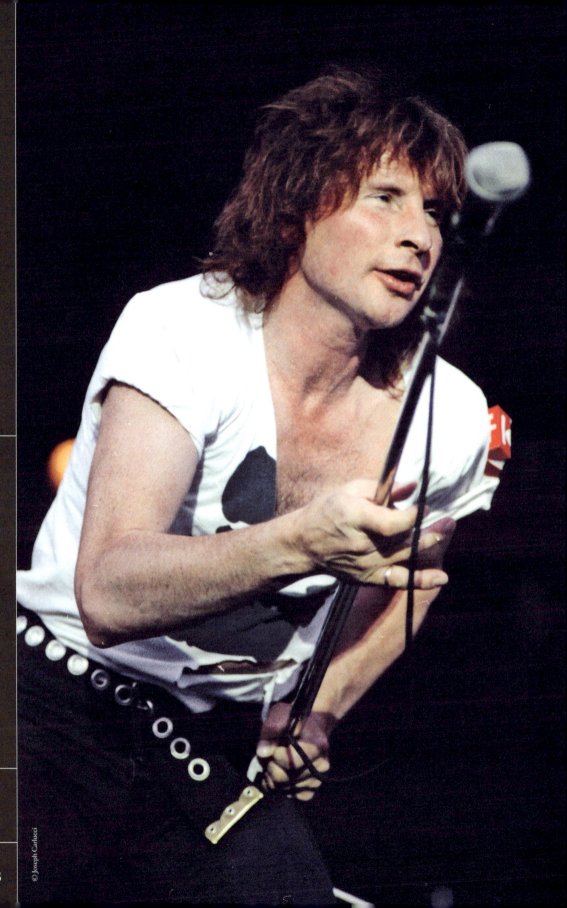

Our third go-around got boycotted by the big shot promotors in Belgium, so we had to jack up the fees to get the bigger bands. UFO wasn't really at the top of their game at the time, but we still shelled out 1.1 million francs for them. And thanks to some shady agency deals, we had to take Tobruk too. Looking back, we could've easily had Slayer as headliners that year. When we finally got them to Heavy Sound, it was their first time in Europe. There were rumours they might pull out, but when we saw that beat-up van roll in and Tom Araya hop out, we were ecstatic. Slayer was stoked that our crew lent a hand with their gear. They never had that kind of treatment before.

We also tried to get Deep Purple, but to no avail. We offered 3 million francs and even flew to Denmark to negotiate with their manager, Eric Thompson. But he brushed us off. Deep Purple ended up playing in Genk for peanuts. We later found out Thompson was splitting the profits with the promoter, Ludo De Bruyne, without Purple knowing about it. I still think Heavy Sound would've been a way better gig for them. *Luc Waeyaert. Written by Stefan Carlier, Spin City fanzine*

I was at Heavy Sound in '84, but '85 was where it was at for me. I've always been more into that melodic hard rock and metal scene. UFO was the main draw for me in Poperinge. Bummer I missed Crossfire, though. For me, Pretty Maids, Tokyo Blade, Lee Aaron, and Tobruk were the highlights with their killer sets.

A band like Slayer? Not my thing at all, to be honest. Didn't dig their sound. I didn't quite get the hysteria, although a huge part of the audience was definitely there for them. And with this whole thrash and speed metal craze, it felt like some of the established hard rock bands were left out in the cold. But hey, UFO always delivers. They rocked the stage with all their classics. Meanwhile, there were all these rumours floating around about some wild stuff going on in downtown Poperinge. From fights to murders to skeletons in the streets, it was all a bit vague. And when the cops started outnumbering the festival-goers, things got real tense. It was quite clear that a '86 edition would never happen. *Jo Hantel*

UFO

Poperinge

The truth about the grave desecration

There's a lot of crazy stories flying around, but I know what really went down. Time to clear up the myths about that whole grave thing. There were three cemeteries in Poperinge, and we were on guard duty for two of them. But the third one was basically abandoned, just a bunch of old graves. Some of the headstones were loose, and you could peek underneath. So, a few festival-goers got the not-so-bright idea to crack open a coffin and pull out the skeleton. We found the teeth a few yards away.

Now, there's this wild tale going around that they stuck the skeleton on a bike and rode it around town. Total bullshit. The editor of German Metal Hammer magazine even showed me pics taken by the culprits. According to him, those grave-robbers were German. The biggest advance sale came from Duisburg, by the way, where we sold over 1,100 tickets.

But fact is that the police never even bothered to check out the scene. That whole mess with the cemetery is why Heavy Sound bit the dust. After that, only a handful of towns would even let us through their gates.

Now, the mayor of Poperinge at the time, Marc Mahieu, he was pretty chill about the whole thing. But the opposition, led by Henri d'Udekem d'Acoz, Queen Mathilde's uncle, used it to score political points. They started this whole paranoia among the locals.

And after the fest, there were rumours that the market square got trashed, but really, only like twenty beer glasses were broken. We agreed to pay the bill for any damage, but some folks tried to milk it for all it was worth. One kid who had an accident with his dad's car, claimed that some festival-goers had wrecked it. So, before the event, we toured Poperinge with the mayor, making a list of everything that was already messed up, just so they couldn't pin it on us later.

If we hadn't been shut down after that third year, we could've brought the bill of Germany's Monsters of Rock to Belgium in 1986. We were already in talks. But in the end, Dynamo Open Air swooped in and stole our thunder. *Luc Waeyaert. Written by Stefan Carlier, Spin City fanzine*

POPERINGE
HEAVY SOUND FESTIVAL
26 MAY 1985

BACKSTAGE na 20 u.

NAME
fTION

POPERINGE
HEAVY SOUND FESTIVAL
26 MAY 1985

BACKSTAGE

NAME

fTION

POPERINGE
HEAVY SOUND FESTIVAL
26 MAY 1985

SECURITY

NAME
fTION

POPERINGE
HEAVY SOUND FESTIVAL
26 MAY 1985

SERVICE

NAME
fTION
N°

POPERINGE
HEAVY SOUND FESTIVAL
26 MAY 1985

SECURITY

NAME
fTION

POPERINGE
HEAVY SOUND FESTIVAL
26 MAY 1985

SECURITY

NAME

fTION

POPERINGE
HEAVY SOUND FESTIVAL
26 MAY 1985

SERVICE

NAME
fTION
N°

POPERINGE
HEAVY SOUND FESTIVAL
26 MAY 1985

SERVICE

NAME
fTION
N°

POPERINGE
HEAVY SOUND FESTIVAL
26 MAY 1985

SERVICE

NAME
fTION
N°

HEAVY SOUND FESTIVAL

MAY 26 1985
POPERINGE · BEL.

CAR
PASS

AAN DE VOORRUIT BEVESTIGEN
MUST BE AFFIXED TO WINDSCREEN

POPERINGE
HEAVY SOUND FESTIVAL
26 MAY 1985

BACKSTAGE

NAME LEE AARON

fTION CREW

POPERINGE
HEAVY SOUND FESTIVAL
26 MAY 1985

SERVICE

FIRMA :

NAME :

POPERINGE
26 MAY 1985

WRITING PRESS

NAME

FTION

POPERINGE
26 MAY 1985

SERVICE

FIRMA :

NAME :

POPERINGE
26 MAY 1985

MEDEWERKER
OP
ZATERDAG

name :

POPERINGE
26 MAY 1985

V.I.P.

ALL AREAS

POPERINGE
26 MAY 1985

SECURITY

NAME :

FTION

POPERINGE
26 MAY 1985

ORGANISATOR

NAME :

POPERINGE
26 MAY 1985

PHOTO PRESS

NAME :

FTION

POPERINGE
26 MAY 1985

GUEST

NAME :

FTION

HEAVY SOUND

26-5-1985

RESTAURANT

good for 1 hot meal

HEAVY SOUND
Luc WAEYAERT
Populiereweg 79
8280 KOEKELARE

medewerker

HEAVY SOUND
Luc WAEYAERT
Populiereweg 79
8280 KOEKELARE

NAME

FUNCTION

NR

POPERINGE
HEAVY SOUND FESTIVAL
26 MAY 1985

T·SHIRT

NAME

FUNCTION

HEAVY SOUND
Luc WAEYAERT
Populiereweg 79
8280 KOEKELARE

NR.

HEAVY SOUND FESTIVAL
26-5-85

HEAVY SOUND FESTIVAL
26 MEI 1985

DRANKBON

WAARDE: 30 F

ENKEL VOOR PERSONEEL

DE NIEUWE **AARDSCHOK** Geert 9

KEIHARD ROCKBLAD...VERSCHIJNT MAANDELIJKS
PRIJS: FL 4,50...BF 90

HEAVY SOUND FESTIVAL

NASTY SAVAGE

POSTER: SLAYER

HALLOWS EVE

WARRIOR RISING FORCE

YRIEMELPOP

LIZZY BORDEN

ODIN

NR. 24 JUN/JUL 85

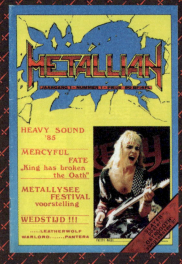

METALLIAN JAARGANG 1 - NUMMER 1 - PRIJS BF 90 BF/4 FL

HEAVY SOUND '85

MERCYFUL FATE „King has broken the Oath"

METALLYSEE FESTIVAL voorstelling

WEDSTIJD !!!

...LEATHERWOLF
WARLORD.......PANTERA

WHIPLASH NR 5 80 FR/4 FL

THOR
ACCEPT
EXCITER
HEAVY SOUND
METAL CHURCH
EARTHQUAKE 85

LEE AARON   SLAYER   WARLOCK

STEEL SHOCK
HARD ROCK & HEAVY METAL

SEPTEMBER 85
40 BFR

METAL BATTLE

POSTER
KEEL
interviews
R.I.P.,
Trial,
Waxfaxe

HEAVY SOUND

ENGLISH METAL

US IMPORT

KEEL
HELLOWEEN
TOKYO BLADE
GRAVE DIGGER
OSTROGOTH
WARRANT,...

SLAYER

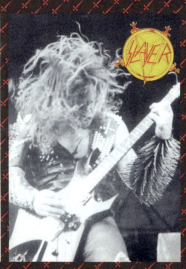

SLAYER

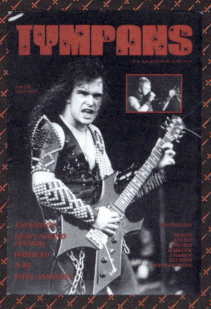

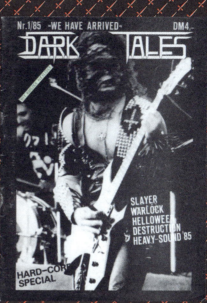

✝✝✝✝✝✝✝

The final countdown

As the bell tolls for Heavy Sound, the festival has a hard time shaking off its grave-robbing associations. But the bells also chime for the birth of a vibrant Flemish metal scene.

379

An unstoppable metal force

Death, resurrection, zombies, and skeletons - metal has always been packed with hellish imagery and rebirth. So, it's no shocker that the party doesn't end with Heavy Sound. Luc Waeyaert and the crew would gear up for another string of gigs. Maeke-Blyde is still shaking to its core with bands like Saxon, Motörhead, and the kick-ass Belgians of Cyclone. And let's not forget Manowar's triumphant return in '86. But still, it's a dwindling tale. The scene seems to be moving beyond its roots. However, this isn't the end - it's just a new beginning. In the late '80s, the rise of hair metal injected some serious cash into the game. Even now, the mix of heavy and glam fuels heated debates among metalheads. And let's not forget its massive impact on the mainstream music scene. Bon Jovi shot to the stars, and suddenly, hard rock - albeit in a diluted form - was blasting from every radio station. Even old-school acts like the Scorpions, KISS, and Aerosmith got a new lease of life. For some, though, it felt like a temporary death knell for the genre, as proven by the many anti-hair metal discussions in fanzines.

Counterculture

Thrash metal, led by legends like Slayer and Metallica, was like a wrecking ball smashing down old barriers, bringing Belgian acts like Cyclone in their fiery wake. It paved the way for new sub-genres like death and black metal, which pushed boundaries even further. Heavy Sound birthed a whole new world of music. Metal isn't just some niche thing anymore; it's huge, like rock and pop.

↓↓↓↓↓↓↓↓↓↓↓↓↓

Thrash metal, led by legends like Slayer and Metallica, was like a wrecking ball smashing down old barriers, bringing Belgian acts like Cyclone in their fiery wake.

↓↓↓↓↓↓↓↓↓↓↓↓↓

Metal's impact on our culture, especially the rebellious side, is massive. In some way, it all started with those 'parental advisory' stickers. Metal was everything that went against the norm, freaking out devoutly religious Americans and thrilling teenagers everywhere. And back in the day, Iron Maiden's Eddie may have looked scary, but compared to today's album covers, his evil gaze has become harmless. Metal's imagery has been copied everywhere, from fashion to mainstream culture. You've got metal bands hitting it big, with Metallica shirts even popping up in stores like H&M. It's all blatantly commercial, but the genre's widespread influence can no longer be denied.

One man's death...

Since the very first Heavy Sound fest back in '83, Bob Schoenmaekers was like a superspreader for the metal virus, especially in the Eastern part of Belgium. This guy sold tickets, shirts, posters, patches - you name it – to local metalheads and way beyond. Plus, he sorted out a shuttle bus to get folks to where the metal mayhem was happening. Bob was like the metal ambassador of the Kempen region, and he clicked with the Heavy Sound crew right away. They practically adopted him as their own, welcoming him backstage and even letting him crash at Luc Waeyaert's place for a week leading up to the last fest.

It was just a taste of what was to come for the new metal hotspot after Heavy Sound: Graspop Metal Meeting in Dessel. When Heavy Sound folded, Bob knew he had something special brewing. He kicked off the Biebob music club in

Vosselaar, where all the big names in international metal would roll through over the years. And not long after that, he set up the indoor Midsummer Metal Meeting. Bob learned a ton from his Heavy Sound days—it was like a masterclass in metal. He saw how the tight-knit metal community worked, but also experienced the chaos and ripping headaches that came with organising events first-hand.

Finally, in '96, he teamed up with Peter Van Geel, who originally started Graspop without a metal vibe. It was your mainstream Flemish festival, think Joe Cocker, Simple Minds and the like. But when Peter saw the crowd numbers dropping, he flipped the script and went all-out metal. After linking up with Bob, the festival got a serious makeover and the first metal edition, with Iron Maiden, Slayer, and Channel Zero, smashed it out of the park. A slice of Heavy Sound history that still resonates today.

Heavy Sound's unfortunate demise was a bummer, but the unstoppable force of metal was a blessing for humanity. The list of killer albums and shows is endless and it still rages on today. And as Belgians, we can beat ourselves on the chest with pride seeing bands like Amenra, Brutus, and Stake making waves internationally (and yep, two of them are from West Flanders). Heavy Sound's influence on our Western region should not be underestimated, its echoes still resonate across Flanders fields.

Vilvoorde-based thrashers Cyclone hold the bragging rights as the only Belgian band to kick off shows for both Metallica (at Forest National on 7 February) and Slayer (at the Brielpoort in Deinze on 1 May) back in 1987.

Manowar - Hail to Europe 1986

My mum and I were all set for a chill night at home when Jacques Merlevede and my stepdad rang us up. Turns out, there were still some tickets left for Manowar, so we decided to tag along. It was super last-minute. I don't remember much about Bad Lizard, they did their thing but couldn't quite win over my younger self with their dodgy sound and static stage act. But soon smoke machines started oozing, filling the hall with a thick, sinister fog. Meanwhile, my stepdad was doing laps with trays piled high with beers, like we were dehydrating or something. I thought it was a bit goofy until a drunken metalhead accidentally knocked stepdad's tray over during the intro. The metal tray and like ten beers hit the floor. And all this with Manowar blasting at full volume! The two of them ended up having a quarrel, not understanding a word of what the other was saying. It was pretty hilarious.

Manowar came out all decked in leather and fur, and being a fan of all things Conan the Barbarian, I was totally into it. The band was dripping with macho vibes, but they put on one hell of a show. Since the shirts they sold were way too big for puny me, my mum bought me a white tour scarf instead. After the gig, we hung out, and the tray-hitter and my stepdad got pretty hammered. What started off with some drama, ended with nothing but love and camaraderie. Good times indeed. *Hans Verbeke*

A young Hans Verbeke with stepfather Johan

For the final round of Heavy Sound, I camped out in Luc Waeyaert's attic for a week. We were all hands on deck, doing everything from plastering posters to setting up the stage. I'll never forget leaving the festival ground in Luc's old Volkswagen Beetle, towing a trailer with a sturdy army-style box strapped to it. Inside? All the cash from the drink stands at the festival. Off we roared to the bank, making sure that the fest's finances were safe and sound. *Bob Schoenmaekers (pictured left)*

For a moment the pilot light starts flickering again. Plans for a fourth edition of the Heavy Sound festival in '87 are on the table. The crew is in talks with several possible locations and organises the Heavy Sound Flashback in Koekelare. After a retrospective slide show, highly popular Belgian band Cyclone blast out the visitors' earwax with their aggressive brand of thrash. Printed at the bottom of the poster, in bold lettering: 'HEAVY SOUND FESTIVAL 4 IS COMING UP'. While the posters get printed, the organisation is still looking to the future with great optimism. But at the time of the actual Flashback event, all talks with new locations have already fallen through. There would never be a fourth edition.

DATE	ARTIST	SUPPORT	FESTIVAL	VENUE	CITY
01/02/1975	Kleptomania			De Gilde	Poperinge
23/03/1975	Amazing Blondel	Zon		De Gilde	Poperinge
12/04/1975	Kandahar	Atlantic Right Whale		De Gilde	Poperinge
25/10/1975	Kayak	Kaz Lux		Maeke-Blyde	Poperinge
27/12/1975	Banzai	Stormy Monday		De Gilde	Poperinge
16/04/1976	Earth & Fire	Pluto		Maeke-Blyde	Poperinge
06/06/1976	KISS			Ontmoetingscentrum	Harelbeke
11/09/1976	Ted Nugent			Ontmoetingscentrum	Harelbeke
16/10/1976	Camel			Maeke-Blyde	Poperinge
31/10/1976	Kayak	Bintangs		Zuudhove	Koekelare
31/10/1976	UFO			Ontmoetingscentrum	Harelbeke
20/11/1976	Focus	Recompensa		Maeke-Blyde	Poperinge
18/11/1976	Tangerine Dream			Ontmoetingscentrum	Harelbeke
22/01/1977	Todd Rundgren			Ontmoetingscentrum	Harelbeke
19/02/1977	Scorpions			Ontmoetingscentrum	Harelbeke
11/03/1977	Van der Graaf Generator	Alquin		Maeke-Blyde	Poperinge
24/4/1977	Pat Travers Band			Belfort	Poperinge
08/10/1977	AC/DC			Belfort	Poperinge
04/12/1977	The Runaways	P.I.G.Z.		Maeke-Blyde	Poperinge
21/01/1978	Scorpions (cancelled)			Maeke-Blyde	Poperinge
27/03/1978	Richie Havens	Josh White Junior		Belfort	Poperinge
04/05/1978	Van Halen	St. James infirmary		Maeke-Blyde	Poperinge
27/10/1978	AC/DC			Koekelaarse Sporthal	Koekelare
27/10/1978	Van Halen (cancelled)			Koekelaarse Sporthal	Koekelare
11/11/1978	Camel			Maeke-Blyde	Poperinge
11/11/1978	Caravan (cancelled)			Maeke-Blyde	Poperinge
18/05/1979	Rush	Max Webster		Maeke-Blyde	Poperinge
04/11/1979	REO Speedwagon			Maeke-Blyde	Poperinge
21/03/1980	Motörhead			Maeke-Blyde	Poperinge
05/04/1980	Turbo		Wheelpop festival	Hallen	Kortrijk
05/04/1980	Ganafoul		Wheelpop festival	Hallen	Kortrijk
05/04/1980	Mc Kitty		Wheelpop festival	Hallen	Kortrijk
05/04/1980	Ian Gillan Band		Wheelpop festival	Hallen	Kortrijk
05/04/1980	Iron Maiden		Wheelpop festival	Hallen	Kortrijk
05/04/1980	Judas Priest (was replaced by Nazareth)		Wheelpop festival	Hallen	Kortrijk
11/10/1980	Girlschool	Toothpaste		Belfort	Poperinge
18/10/1980	Golden Earring	Once More, Jardon Lane		Beurshalle	Brugge
25/04/1981	Rose Tattoo			Maeke-Blyde	Poperinge
05/12/1981	Killer	Buzzard, The Raves		Maeke-Blyde	Poperinge
28/01/1982	Gillan			Maeke-Blyde	Poperinge
29/01/1982	Tygers of Pan Tang			Maeke-Blyde	Poperinge

	ARTIST	SUPPORT	FESTIVAL	VENUE	CITY
04/06/1982	Venom	Acid		Maeke-Blyde	Poperinge
19/02/1983	Def Leppard			Maeke-Blyde	Poperinge
06/02/1983	UFO	Spider		Maeke-Blyde	Poperinge
03/04/1983	Accept	Savage		Maeke-Blyde	Poperinge
23/04/1983	Frank Marino & Mahogany Rush			Maeke-Blyde	Poperinge
21/05/1983	Ostrogoth		Heavy Sound	Football stadium of Cercle Brugge	
21/05/1983	Viva		Heavy Sound	Football stadium of Cercle Brugge	
21/05/1983	Golden Earring		Heavy Sound	Football stadium of Cercle Brugge	
21/05/1983	Killer		Heavy Sound	Football stadium of Cercle Brugge	
21/05/1983	Warning		Heavy Sound	Football stadium of Cercle Brugge	
21/05/1983	Anvil		Heavy Sound	Football stadium of Cercle Brugge	
21/05/1983	Uriah Heep		Heavy Sound	Football stadium of Cercle Brugge	
21/05/1983	Gary Moore		Heavy Sound	Football stadium of Cercle Brugge	
21/05/1983	Barón Rojo		Heavy Sound	Football stadium of Cercle Brugge	
22/10/1983	Viva		Abasti	Zuudhove	Koekelare
12/02/1984	Venom	Metallica		Maeke-Blyde	Poperinge
24/03/1984	Gary Moore			d'oude sporthal	Zwevegem
10/06/1984	H Bomb		Heavy Sound	Don Bosco sportzone	Poperinge
10/06/1984	Faithful Breath		Heavy Sound	Don Bosco sportzone	Poperinge
10/06/1984	Lita Ford		Heavy Sound	Don Bosco sportzone	Poperinge
10/06/1984	Mercyful Fate		Heavy Sound	Don Bosco sportzone	Poperinge
10/06/1984	Manowar (was replaced by Baron Rojo)		Heavy Sound	Don Bosco sportzone	Poperinge
10/06/1984	Metallica		Heavy Sound	Don Bosco sportzone	Poperinge
10/06/1984	Twisted Sister		Heavy Sound	Don Bosco sportzone	Poperinge
10/06/1984	Motörhead		Heavy Sound	Don Bosco sportzone	Poperinge
05/10/1984	Manowar			Maeke-Blyde	Poperinge
24/11/1984	Marillion			Maeke-Blyde	Poperinge
17/11/1984	Metallica	Tank		Maeke-Blyde	Poperinge
01/12/1984	Exocet			Schuttershof	St Kruis Brugge
25/01/1985	Tokyo Blade			Maeke-Blyde	Poperinge
24/03/1985	Uli J. Roth's Electric Sun	Robin George		Maeke-Blyde	Poperinge
26/05/1985	Crossfire		Heavy Sound	Sportzone	Poperinge
26/05/1985	Warlock		Heavy Sound	Sportzone	Poperinge
26/05/1985	Lee Aaron		Heavy Sound	Sportzone	Poperinge
26/05/1985	Tokyo Blade		Heavy Sound	Sportzone	Poperinge
26/05/1985	Pretty Maids		Heavy Sound	Sportzone	Poperinge
26/05/1985	Tobruk		Heavy Sound	Sportzone	Poperinge
26/05/1985	Slayer		Heavy Sound	Sportzone	Poperinge
26/05/1985	UFO		Heavy Sound	Sportzone	Poperinge
06/10/1985	Alaska			belfort	Poperinge
04/04/1986	Manowar	Bad Lizard		Maeke-Blyde	Poperinge

Earthquake Heavy Sound: Aftershocks way into 2024

In my teenage years, I devoured music media like there was no tomorrow. Every week, I'd snag the latest Humo magazine and dug straight to the back for the reviews, starting with the ones reviewed with the most stars. I'd memorise those highly rated gems for my next trip to the LP Centre in Waregem, where I would get personal CD listening sessions at the counter. And on weekends, after drum class, you could find me at the library, poring over every page of the Dutch OOR magazine.

It was only a matter of time before I picked up the digital pen myself. After dabbling in a few student magazines, I started freelancing as a reviewer and interviewer for Humo and Red Bull Music. It was through the latter that I got schooled on the rich metal history of the Westhoek. Those Heavy Sound interviews were packed with badass band names; the Belgian acts back then sounded menacing and fierce. But little did I know what was in store just a few years down the road.

In January 2024, I got a message from Hans Verbeke, who I didn't know at the time. He hit me up about working on a book about the Heavy Sound Festival. I have to admit, I was a bit skeptical at first. A whole book about some local festival? But Hans was so fired up about it, I couldn't help but get on board. So, a little later, we're sitting in a café, and the book's designer Onno Hesselink busts out the first draft. The guy had gathered up a mountain of epic photos, plus photocopies of posters, ticket stubs, you name it. The stories were captivating. Who would've thought future rock legends from all corners of the globe gave it their all at some local sports field?

Being a country kid from Anzegem myself, I could easily picture what a metal fest would bring to rural West Flanders. That sense of local flavour, mixed with grit and a deep love for the music - it all paints a beautiful picture. And I think this book captures it perfectly. Personally, it's given me a newfound respect for the old metal gods. I got into the genre through young Belgian acts like Steak Number Eight, Raketkanon, and Amenra. That was around the time Metallica dropped 'Lulu', which wasn't exactly a crowd-pleaser. But when I imagine 'Fight Fire With Fire' echoing like an air raid over the Westhoek, I can easily imagine the relentless impact of those four pimple-faced teenagers.

And so, after forty years, Heavy Sound is once again making waves, reigniting the metal flame and drawing us all in with excitement. It might go against the typical West Flemish modesty, but I'll boldly say, we've done a darn good job. This book acts as a time machine, transporting us back to that incredible era. But let's not forget, the real heroes are the ones who booked the bands, organised the gigs, fixed things on the fly, volunteered their time and effort, poured pints, built stages, and so much more. They took nothing and turned it into something extraordinary. They fueled their creation with passion, and ignited it with a bang that echoed throughout the region. Though I wasn't there in person, I'm grateful for their initiative and unwavering spirit! *Zeno Van Moerkerke*

Hans Verbeke is a punk, hardcore, and metal fanatic. He grew up in Kortrijk, West Flanders, soaking in the vibes of the 70s and 80s subcultures. Hans played in epic bands like Nations on Fire, Blindfold, and LIAR. After dropping 'The Story of H8000 Hardcore' in 2019, 'Heavy Sounds In The West' is the second musical reference work he is involved in. Hans lives in Kortrijk with his wife Hilde and their two dogs and two cats.

Onno Hesselink is a punk/hardcore scene vet and graphic designer who rocked the 80s with his fanzine 'Peace or Annihilation'. His love for tunes started early when he got The Osmonds' 'Crazy Horses' single for his seventh birthday, and he's been hooked ever since. Onno's whipped up over 300 record covers for big labels like Good Life Recordings and Lowlands. Fresh out of school, he even did the cover for Cyclone's second LP 'Inferior to None'. Originally from Zandvoort, Netherlands, he's kickin' it now in Tervuren, Belgium.

Zeno Van Moerkerke is a music junkie in heart, kidneys and neck muscles. Back in the day, he devoured every music review in Dutch and practically camped out at the LP Center in Waregem. He's got a knack for writing, which he has flexed in mags like Humo and Indiestyle. Nowadays, he's spreading the music love through Prize Dink Camp, Het Onderspit, and Keurslager Kurt. Originally from Anzegem, he's now swapped it for the Brugse Poort in Ghent.

393

The legacy of Popcenter: Metal education under the Broeltowers

Jacques Merlevede, second from right

On January 11, 2024, Kortrijk bid farewell to a true legend, Jacques Merleve-de. His name will forever be intertwined with Popcenter, a record shop known as the musical epicenter of West Flanders and beyond. Popcenter leaves behind a treasure trove of memories and an irreplaceable void following its closure. Jacques introduced his community to the gritty sounds of hard rock, metal, and punk - a legacy etched into the very walls of the old Popcenter on the Burgemeester Reynaertstraat. But Jacques did much more than just sell music; he ignited a passion in generations and left a permanent mark on the region's musical landscape. His legacy serves as a timeless reminder of an era when Popcenter wasn't just a store, but a haven of musical exploration and defiance. While its physical closure may mark the end, its influence lives on in the hearts of all who ever set foot into this musical institution. *Hans Verbeke*

Text credits:
historischekranten.be, Johan 'Amedee' Pauwels

Photo credits:
PG Brunelli, Joseph Carlucci, Paul Coerten - www.rockpictures.be, Rudy De Doncker,
Carl De Keyzer, Stephan Mandeville, Frederick Moulaert, Piet Overstijns, Pierre
Terrasson, Poperinge stadsarchief, Archief Eric Deroo, Westhoek verbeeldt - privécollectie
And last but not least: endless gratitude for the many photos we received, without a
name on them. Your contributions really helped us shape this book.

Concept: Hans Verbeke & Onno Hesselink
Ghostwriter: Zeno Van Moerkerke
English translation: Chris Dexters
Design: Onno Hesselink & Els Vandecan, www.els-onno.be
Color separations: Onno Hesselink
© 2024, heavyreads.com

Thanks to Dave Skinner, Ann Welter, Rudy De Doncker, Frederick Moulaert, Luc
Waeyaert, Guido Gevels and to everyone who contributed something essential to
make this piece of work as complete as possible. You all fucking rule.

HEAVY SOUND FEST GEEN NODELOZ

POPERINGE. - Op zondag 10 juni (Sinksen) vanaf 11 u. heeft te Poperinge het Heavy Sound Festival plaats op de Don Bosco-sportzone. De laatste paar dagen wordt over praktisch niets anders meer gepraat dan over de circa 7.000 «headbangers» die zondag hun tenten in Poperinge zullen opslaan. Poperinge is ongerust, ja zelfs bang. Ten onrechte.

«Wat voor een streek is dat hier?» vroegen de organisatoren van het festival zich af. «Iedereen lijkt verschrikt.» «We zijn inderdaad maar gewoon te luisteren naar een koe die loeit», antwoordde een Poperi...

een speciaal getraind security-team. IJzeren voorwerpen blikjes en... drugs worden afgenomen. Eens gefouilleerd, en dat laten de headbangers goedlachs ge...

POPERINGE. - Als er nog een Heavy Sound festival komt, dan zal dat zeker niet meer in Poperinge doorgaan»: dat is de konklusie van de organisatoren na de derde editie van dat festival... in Poperinge plaatshad. De... peringenaar zal daar waarschijnlijk niet... uren, maar toch moet een ander verduide-...

Vervolg zie blz 15

bleke opkomst als qua nu... ziek Zeker dat laatst...
zjaar Zowel qua pu-

VERLEG UW GRENZEN

...tart en Annemie Decuyper kiezen samen met... uit een gevarieerd aanbod de reis van uw

---

POPERINGE 2

HEAVY METAL KLANK IN DE GEMEENTERAAL

POPERINGE. - De relletjes en incidenten die er tijdens het voorbije Heavy Sound Festival in Poperinge zijn geweest, kwamen ook - zoals verwacht - ter sprake in de gemeenteraadszitting van maandag ll. De gemeenteraad begon er zelfs mee. Later, tijdens de diskussies over andere punten, waren er ook heavy metal klanken te horen. Verbaal, maar - gelukkig - geen fysiek geweld.

Bij de aanvang van de gemeenteraadszitting vroeg raadslid d'Udekem het woord om een verklaring af te leggen in verband met de «wandaden» gepleegd tijdens het Heavy Sound Festival. Ook burgemeester Mahieu wou een verklaring afleggen daaromtrent. De burgemeester zei dat hij, na de politiekommissaris gehoord te hebben over de feiten, en na het drama op de Heizel, zich persoonlijk besloten had dat zo'n festival in Poperinge geen doorgang meer kon vinden. «Ik heb het al aan de pers verklaard», aldus de burgemeester, «vooraleer... wil ik de offi-...

OPPOSITIEVERKLARING

Volgens mr. d'Udekem wilde de tolk zijn van het overgrote gedeelte van de Poperinge bevolking. De fraktie was verwonderd dat er na de eerste festival toch een toelating gegeven werd voor een tweede organisatie: «Het moet voor u toch duidelijk geweest zijn dat de ekonomische en kulturele voordelen van zo'n festival niet opwegen tegen de schade die de bevolking daarbij lijdt. Waarom dan opnieuw een toelating verleend en waarom werd dat gespuis nogmaals als gasten ontvangen?»

d'Udekem wilde ook nog weten welke garanties er aan organisatoren gegeven werden op...

hof in de Deken Debolaan waar was. «Als dat effektief ist is, dan is het een ware sc... zulke kriminelen op h... gebied en in hun... werden verhinderd...

De spreker vro... waarom er geen... werden genomen... te verhinderen... dagnacht, nad... voormiddag... dat er al kun... «Waarom w... lasting van... tiekorps gr... de rijks... Provinci... ze bew... voeren...

POLITIEKE REL NA HEAVY SOU

POPERINGE. - Op zondag 26 mei had in Poperinge voor de tweede keer een Heavy Sound Festival plaats. Dat festival dreunt in Poperinge nog zwaar na op politiek vlak. Zoals u op een andere plaats in Het Wekelijks Nieuws kunt lezen is er een fikse politieke rel ontstaan tussen schepenkollege en CVP-oppositieleider Henri d'Udekem. Het schepenkollege verdenkt de... schennis. Hoe...

Het Heavy Sound-... Poperinge is voorbij... 8.000 festivalgan-... gers genaamd, trokken...

Veertig t.h. van hen waren landers. In overgrote meerde... landers, Britten, Franse... Duitsers. Nu raamt de gr... haar schade. Nu raamt de grens... nog mee te vallen, zie... zijn de leek aanvanke... wordt die gebeuren overschadig... wordt door een gevo...

UFO als top of the bill

Heavy Sound Festival minder hard

POPERINGE – Ondanks allerlei klachten betreffende schade, kunnen de headbangers zich nu al verkneukelen in de derde uitgave van het Heavy Sound Festival dat zich op zondag 26 mei onder Poperingse openlucht moet voltrekken. Op de affiche staan eens te meer acht groepen met als hoofdact de oude glorie UFO met „atomic" Tommy als vervanger van de legendarische Michael Schenker. Op de Amerikaanse speedmetal band Slayer na, is de programmatie minder „hard" in vergelijking met de vorige uitgaven. Maar nog steeds hard genoeg.

„Je mag je niet blind staren op die schade-geruchten," vertelt Luc Waeyaert, samen met Rik Staal verantwoordelijk voor de organisatie van het festival. „Er was natuurlijk wel schade maar die was vooral veroorzaakt door enkele Duitsers en zo erg was het nu ook weer niet: de viering van de laatste „100 dagen" van

Deep Purple via andere organizatoren naar België, gewoon omdat de mensen elkaar beter kennen. We worden nog steeds beschouwd als zijnde een klein festivalletje en daardoor zijn onze problemen legio. Oorspronkelijk zouden we een pakket van vier groepen hebben gebracht waaronder ook Judas P... en Ozzy Osborne maar...

gedraagt. En dat zijn dan nog meestal buitenlanders. In principe zijn we klaar om 20.000 mensen op te vangen dus de verwachte 8.000 kunnen geen probleem zijn."

De geïnteresseerden zijn waarschijnlijk al op de hoogte maar voor de volledigheid zetten we de aantredende groepen nog eens op een rijtje. Vanaf

MERCERIE

fem...